Creative Children's Parties

by
Allison Boteler

BARRON'S

Credits
Color photography by Thom De Santo Photography Inc.
Food Styling by Andrea Swenson
Photo styling by Debrah E. Donahue
Illustrated by Pamela Carroll

In loving memory of my father, William Connett Boteler

All inquiries should be addressed to:
Barron's Educational Series, Inc.
250 Wireless Boulevard
Hauppauge, New York 11788
http://www.barronseduc.com

International Standard Book No.: 0-7641-0881-6

Library of Congress Catalog Card No: 99-62852

Printed in Hong Kong
9 8 7 6 5 4 3 2

TABLE OF CONTENTS

INTRODUCTION

A party is one of the most precious gifts that a parent can give a child. Although it lasts only a few hours, the memories will last for a lifetime. Long after the toys are broken, worn, lost, or simply forgotten, warm fuzzy thoughts about "My birthday party when . . . " will always linger. As soon as children are old enough to eat ice cream and put on a paper hat, they're ready for the magical world of birthday parties.

This book is designed for parents looking to create an afternoon of original fantasy and fun, the kind you just can't find in a fast-food chain. That doesn't mean you have to go to the other extreme and become "Super Mom" or "Super Dad." Everything from the invitations and decorations to the cake and ice cream are simply suggestions to spur your own imagination. The party experience should never be about throwing the biggest bash you can possibly afford or knocking yourself out to do everything from scratch. That's not what your child really wants or needs. Your child wants and needs to share this milestone day in a way that bonds both of you. No matter what your schedule, everyone's a working parent. Time is precious, and no one ever seems to have enough. If the thought of throwing a birthday party intimidates you . . . relax. Simply do what you can. In fact, that's my motto throughout this book. Don't feel overwhelmed by all of the ideas and projects; just pick and choose the elements that you want to use. On the other hand, I can guarantee you'll start having so much fun that everything will seem much easier than you ever imagined.

Type of Party

The two determining factors in deciding what type of party to give your child are age and interest. What entertains a child of 3 will change dramatically by the time he or she is 7 years old. Gender

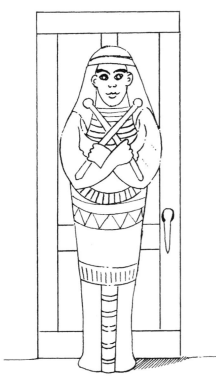

also plays a role, but not as much as you might think. Many themes are universal, like teddy bears, dinosaurs, or aliens. Others are not as clear-cut. For example, my brother had a pirate party, and I had to be a pirate too. On the other hand, you won't find many little boys wanting to be an Egyptian princess or have a cruise ship slumber party. Chances are, your child has already cast a vote for the next party theme. Kids' interests change rapidly. What's popular with the peer group one year may be totally dead by the next. Fads come and go and are soon forgotten. Of course, movies, heroes, cartoons, and toys have their influence on each generation.

The problem is that they can be completely "burned out" if they're the same subject at everyone's party. There are also timeless themes that will always be good, and many that transcend age differences. Some of these are educational as well, and will actually encourage your child to research the topic. This book focuses on both classic and contemporary themes that are unlikely to be "in" one year and "out" the next.

How Many, Where, and When?

Size is another important consideration. As the guest list increases, so do food and material costs . . . not to mention stress. Your ability to control the situation diminishes with each additional child. Never attempt to throw a kids' party on your own. It's you against an army of busy little bodies. Always recruit the aid of other parents, friends, neighbors, or relatives. For toddlers, it's standard practice to include at least one parent per child as guest. The advantages to this arrangement are obvious. As kids grow older, there are many "formulas" used for party size. One says to add a child for each year of age. Another says to use the age plus 2 extra kids. Of course, all of this goes out the window if you have a long list of party payback obligations. For practical purposes, I've used the magic number of a dozen to gauge the projects and recipes in this book. Twelve is a manageable number (with the help of additional adults), and it really is necessary to have enough guests for many games to even get rolling.

How long should a party last from start to finish? Toddlers tire after an hour and a half (if that long). The average grade-school party should last about 2 hours, with some exceptions. Outdoor parties and parties with lengthy craft activities can go on all afternoon, especially if the guests are in the 9- to 10-year-old range. Of course, slumber parties are marathon events.

Indoors or out? Well, wouldn't we all like to be able to predict the weather! Anyone who's ever had a washed-out garden wedding, or had to cancel a trip because a blizzard kept them from getting out to the airport, knows the frustration. With children's parties, "Murphy's Law" usually applies. Never make your plans dependent on being outdoors unless you have a rain-check date or an alternate arrangement to move everything inside. That doesn't mean you can't plan a party at a park, playground, or beach. You just have to be sure that there are sheltered facilities at your disposal and that they won't be crowded with other parties presented with the same weather woes. (It's kind of like being on a sinking ship without enough lifeboats.) There are pros and cons to away vs.

at-home parties. If you hold your party at another facility, you spare your house a lot of mess—or you don't have to clean up a mess getting ready for the party. On the other hand, kids take personal pride in having their friends come to "their house" on "their day." It makes them feel like king in their castle.

(Depending on your child's personality, this can be either good or bad.) I describe the parties in this book as home celebrations simply because this idea gives you so many creative possibilities for decorations and games.

When is the best time to have the party? Back when I was a kid, it was customary to hold parties as afternoon affairs on the actual day of the birthday. Refreshments of cake and ice cream were served and we played a couple of games. Just as with scout meetings, everyone was back home by dinner—granted, no one felt like eating again. As I grew older, kids wanted to eat lunch or dinner at parties. In the case of slumber parties, we wanted to eat all night long!

Things have changed somewhat. Now that so many parents are working, everyone seems to have their child's birthday on either the weekend before or after the actual date. This often presents the heart-breaking problem of competing parties. When two kids are born during the same week, their birthday parties should never escalate into a popularity contest. It can be psychologically devastating. (I remember when *The Dick Van Dyke Show* used this as a classic theme.) As soon as you're aware of a schedule conflict, contact the other family and try to negotiate. If both of you must have the same date, there are other options that can actually work to your advantage. For example, a progressive party can be planned where the same group of guests starts out at one party and is transported to the other. An alternative would be to pool the parties and all of the preparations that go with it. This often works wonderfully and defrays expense and time involved for both families.

Summer birthdays present another set of problems. How do you celebrate when friends are off on a vacation or away at camp? My poor brother never liked his July birthday for that very reason; we usually ended up with a very small turnout. And thus was born his "unbirthday party." He'd usually pick a holiday, like Halloween, to have a seasonal party. One year we dressed up like Pilgrims and had a mock Thanksgiving dinner on the Friday after Thanksgiving. Parents loved it because they used the day to go shopping.

Age-Appropriate Parties

The prime time for parties is between the ages of 4 and 8. This is when kids are old enough to truly interact with one another but young enough to still consider themselves "children." Kids never lose the desire to have birthday parties; they're just afraid of being judged by their peers. Boys outgrow structured birthdays sooner than girls. An exception is when a party becomes a spoof or parody of something—it then becomes OK to dress up and act silly. This is very liberating to an otherwise "cool" 10 year old.

AGES 1–3

These first birthdays are usually family affairs. A parent should accompany each child and be present through the duration of the party. This helps keep children as calm and contented as possible in an otherwise overstimulating situation. Toddler parties are actually a wonderful opportunity to socialize and share child-rearing experiences with friends and relatives. In many respects, you are entertaining the adult guests at your party. After all, they're the ones who will actually appreciate all of your effort. Keep parties short at this age—about an hour will do. You may just want to have one game and time to eat cake and ice cream.

AGES 4–5

At this age the total concept of "BIRTHDAY" really starts to sink in. Four and 5 year olds are genuinely enthusiastic and accepting of just about any game or activity you present. They are starting to relate to one another and interact in a group setting . . . until they wear each other out. Keeping track of newly acquired property suddenly becomes very important. Hats, favors, and goody bags should all be marked with children's names, or the rightful owners can become very distressed. Eating habits tend to be picky. Don't assume you can even put condiments as simple as ketchup on a burger without some child refusing to eat. Giving this age group small choices is comforting and gives them a sense of control.

AGES 6–8

This is party prime time. These are the years that you and your child will always remember, so you want to make them memorable. Six year olds are starting to plan their party themes from one year to the next. Seven and 8 year olds are actually ready to get involved with many aspects of the party preparations, such as helping with invitations and decorations and even getting their hands into the cake baking. (This can be good or bad for the end result. Remember that it's the bonding experience, not the culinary creation, that counts.) By age 6, competition tends to surface and games can become rowdy. It's important to maintain control. By age 7, kids tend to follow a group with one leader emerging. Depending on the personality of the "leader," this can be a positive influence . . . or chaos! This age group has a growing appetite, so serving a full meal makes sense.

AGES 9–11

By this time, kids are becoming a tough audience to impress. When it comes to party themes, they've "been there and done that." It takes more originality to draw them into the party spirit. Organized games need to be entertaining or they won't cooperate. Winners and prizes are less important than the opportunity to laugh at themselves. By 11, kids are becoming more "grown-up" and critical of contrived activities that they might consider themselves too sophisticated to enjoy. Boys are pretty much past the age of theme parties. Girls can still have a lot of fun, as long as it's on their terms. Slumber parties and parties for holidays like Halloween will always be popular. In this age group, it's important to let your daughter be involved in all of the party details from start to finish.

Party Elements

Whenever possible, include your child in these party preparations. As soon as children are old enough to do art projects in school, they're ready to get involved in the best art project of all . . . their own birthday party. At any age, there's always something they can do, whether it's drawing on the sidewalk, blowing up balloons, helping with the party hats, or writing out the invitations. Older kids may want complete control over the "decorating committee" for their big event. What's important is that it's fun for them . . . not that it's perfect.

THE INVITATION

When you think about it, the invitation really sets the stage for the entire party. It should whet the appetite of your guests for all of the fun that's in store for them. If you're pressed for time, there are always commercially prepared invitations that incorporate traditional themes like "circus," "pirates," and so on. But when it comes to truly unique themes, you're on your own. Not to worry—that's what will make your party special! Did you know there are services in

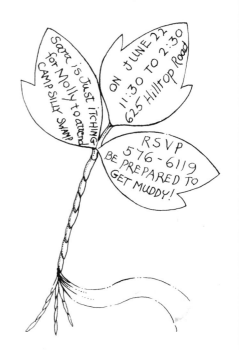

Hollywood that even design custom invitations just for celebrities in your same situation? Many of those soirees are announced with custom-made elements from the movie or book being promoted (such as a miniature model of the *Titanic*). Such invitations can often cost a couple of hundred dollars apiece. So creative invitations aren't just kids' stuff!

Fortunately, homemade invitations are often the most economical way to go. Throughout this book, you will find the invitation to be a simple and enjoyable craft project that your family can share. To make things simpler for you (and avoid writer's cramp), use your home computer or a copier machine whenever you're repeating the same message over and over. This usually applies to the inside message: date, time, address, and special instructions. On the other hand, feel free to "do your own thing" and design your entire invitation on the computer. Explore your software for all of the possibilities.

It's important to send an invitation out about two to three weeks before the event. You want to allow enough time for parents to mark it on their calendars, make any special arrangements, and get in touch with you. I personally do not believe in "Regrets Only." This might be necessary to keep a phone from ringing off the wall prior to a huge gala. However, you're dealing with a children's party and a guest list that probably won't exceed a dozen kids. It's important to have that RSVP so that you make a personal connection with each parent and give any specifics on clothing to wear or what to bring. Remember that some homemade invitations in this book take unusual forms and are best delivered by hand.

DECORATIONS

Decorations are important to any party because they create the scene for a fantasy to take place, much like a movie set. When you first read the laundry list of decoration ideas for each party theme, you may feel overwhelmed. Don't. These are just suggestions for you to pick and choose what best suits your time frame, skills, and budget. Just do whatever you feel like doing. Sometimes something as simple as a sign at the end of the driveway and a special table arrangement is all it takes to get your guests in a magical mood.

PARTY GEAR

Assuming a new identity is part of a theme party experience. That's why this book goes beyond the cone-shaped birthday hat and takes party gear to a whole new level. The projects in this book are easy to make and also double as favors for your guests to take home. Sometimes the kids need to arrive dressed in certain attire to complete the costume. This is usually explained in the invitation or when parents RSVP.

INSTANT INVOLVEMENT

Involving a child the minute he or she walks through the door is the key to a successful party. There's always an awkward period at parties when the first few guests start to arrive (often too early) and the rest have yet to come. For these kids, a positive experience will determine their mood for the hours ahead. In this book, I've suggested activities that will involve children and encourage positive interaction. This is of particular importance in the situation where some guests may have only your child's friendship in common and not know each other. An "instant involvement" activity should be somewhat unstructured so that arriving guests can continuously join in without disruption.

GAMES/ACTIVITIES

No party would be complete without games to entertain and blow off steam. Obviously, some are better suited for outdoors and some for indoors. Most games follow familiar principles, with the theme determining the dynamics. Typical themes are hunting games, hiding games, types of tag, musical chair-rotation games, variants on "Simon Says," piñatas, storytelling, races, and relays. Team-type relay games are among my favorites because they really get kids involved without one-on-one competition. I've suggested three games for every party. You may not have time for all three, or weather and space may determine your choice. Never let kids get stuck in a game that goes on too long. Move on to the next. On the other hand, if everyone is really having a good time, why cut it short?

Don't get too hung up on rules. Rules are meant to be broken. As a child, I remember instances when a game was "dying" until it evolved into something totally different. So what? As long as it's not disruptive, the whole point is having fun. Prizes are often part of the game; however, they're not always necessary. Kids will get their party loot in their goody bags, giving everyone a fair share of the same stuff. One of my favorite ways to pass the time at parties is through noncompetitive arts and crafts-type activities. These draw out the shyest of children and give everyone a souvenir to take home.

GOODY BAGS

Over the years, "goody bags" have become a party prerequisite. It's simply a given that kids are going to get one. They play an important role in appeasing kids who have brought birthday gifts they'd really prefer to keep for themselves. Goody bags help even the exchange. Unfortunately, this is where many parents end up going overboard on their party budget. First of all, try to use your party theme to think creatively. Many times, common

things can be repackaged in an uncommon way. The bags themselves take on a whole new interest when they've been hand-decorated in spirit with the party theme. As far as trinkets and toys are concerned, they really are cheaper by the dozen. In addition to party supply outlets, my favorite resources are Oriental Trading Company, Inc. (call 1-800-228-2269 for a catalog) and Birthday Express (call 1-800-424-7843 for a catalog).

PRESENTS AND POST-PARTY DEPRESSION

For the birthday boy or girl, the pinnacle of the party is opening those anxiously awaited gifts. But with the ups come the downs. Disappointment is almost inevitable when children either don't get what they wanted or get duplicate presents. (This is nothing new— I remember crying about getting four "Beenie Copters" on my sixth birthday!) Every parent should be prepared for the great lows that accompany the highs of this experience. It's only natural for kids to anticipate their party and presents for weeks in advance. This often results in unrealistic ideas of what their family and friends may actually give them. Also, if the party hasn't lived up to your child's expectations, frustration and tears may take over. Even the most glorious parties are usually followed by a transient depression. The mood often sets in halfway through the party with the realization that "all good things must come to an end." For this reason, many parents prefer to save presents for the end of the party. There are advantages to this. It prolongs the mystery while postponing disappointment and broken toys.

A friend of mine has an unconventional approach. She sidesteps the whole package-opening ritual in front of guests. She believes in saving it for after the guests go home. The family spends a special time together, snapping photos of the process to include in the (very important) thank-you notes. Although this flies in the face of tradition, she feels it really avoids a lot of problems and appeases the "party's over" depression. However, most kids are reluctant to give up this custom. My parents had a different approach. Mom always saved a piece of cake and a present to open a few days after my birthday, when we'd begin planning the theme for the following year.

PHOTO OPS AND THANK-YOU NOTES

Since the birth of the camera, birthday parties have been one of the most important events to document on film. These are milestone moments that you'll want to remember for years and years. When I was a kid, Polaroid and 8mm movies were a major technology. Now, with camcorders, you can even get instant replay. Polaroid still has an important role because instant pictures of kids in costumes make fun take-home favors. In every chapter, you'll find suggestions for great photo opportunities so your camera will be ready and waiting. These shots also are thoughtful to include in thank-you notes.

This brings up a subject very close to my heart. I believe that thank-you notes help build a child's character. As much as they may procrastinate and protest, the etiquette will follow them through their personal and professional lives. Learning to be gracious is an invaluable lesson. It's important that you help your child compose sincere and appreciative responses to every guest's gift (even if it bombed!).

MEALS AND MENUS

Throughout this book you'll see complete menu plans for each party theme. These are really meant as suggestions, since you know better than anyone else what your child will eat. I've taken the most popular kid-friendly foods (franks, burgers, pizza, and chicken) and presented them in completely new forms. For example, your average package of hot dogs can be transformed into "Pharaoh Phranks" or "Brontosaurus Bones" with the help of refrigerated breadsticks.

Children's appetites really depend on the age group. For older kids you might want to double recipes to allow for second helpings, whereas toddlers may struggle to finish one "Teddy Bear Burger." In fact, I often think serving cake and ice cream is a simple solution for children under 6. It really depends on the time of day and if you are also feeding the parents. (Moms enjoy your efforts on party food even more than their kids.)

In this book you will find recipes for wholesome fruits and salads to round out meals, although most kids will consider potato chips a vegetable. The older the child, the more he or she will have opinions on what is served. Since it's their party, you should let their tastes be your guide. However, don't miss the opportunity to introduce the peer group to new experiences. Frequently kids will venture out and try something different in a party setting, while they'd just balk at it in front of Dad at the dinner table. Whenever possible, prepare as much as you can the day before the party so you won't feel flustered at the last minute by oven timers or melting ice cream.

It Takes the Cake!

There's no doubt about it, it's not a party without a cake. Most kids expect more on their birthday than two layers with a candle on top. They want it to look like some challenging shape. I've had frantic mothers call me wanting to know how to make anything from a fire engine to a grasshopper. This is really nothing new. I did the same thing to my mom, year after year. Necessity is the mother of invention, and my mom never disappointed me. I learned from her that you can sculpt standard round, square, or rectangular cakes into just about any conceivable shape. This is why I don't believe in buying specialty shaped pans. Your child isn't going to want the same cake over and over again. I once bought a "Wonder Woman" cake pan and later tried to recycle it by turning it into a Santa Claus at Christmas . . . it was a bit of a stretch!

Many of these chapters include recipes for batters and frostings from scratch. Others are just variations on a cake mix and colored canned frosting. Remember that you can always substitute mixes and canned frostings for any theme cake concept. The important thing is that you bake your child's favorite flavor and that you don't stress yourself out. Let's suppose you doubt you have the time and talent to bake a T-rex cake (although I guarantee that it's easy). Buy a cake and put plastic dinosaurs on top. There's no "right way" to throw a party, and there should never be any guilt.

Most people discover that baking party cakes for kids requires less skill than they'd thought. You won't need elaborate equipment, but you will need the following supplies. Most of these can now be purchased at supermarkets without having to even go to a specialty shop. The following supplies are really invaluable, not only for this book, but for any cake you might dream up in the future. Believe me, the more you bake, the more you'll create!

Party Cake Pantry

Pans:

8" and 9" round cake pans
8" and 9" square cake pans
13" x 9" rectangular cake pans
6-cup ring mold pans
9" x 5" loaf pans
muffin pans for cupcakes

Baking Parchment:

This is an absolute must-have, can't-live-without baking essential. Sure, you can grease and flour pans. However, you'll still have to hold your breath when it comes time to invert them and pray they'll come out in one piece. With parchment, the batter rises evenly and the cake is level on top. This avoids cracks. It won't stick to the pan, so you can cool the cake completely in the pan before removing it. Best of all, you barely have to wash the pan when you're done. Baking parchment also saves sugar cookies and gingerbread men from inevitable broken arms and legs.

Wire Cake Racks:
Essential for cooling and inverting cakes.

Rubber Spatulas:
Purchase a set of assorted sizes that are flexible rubber. They're indispensable for scraping batter and frosting bowls.

Metal Spatulas:
Have at least one large and one small angled spatula for spreading and smoothing frostings. Avoid "crumble pox" on your cakes by using a small metal spatula to gently crumb-coat the dry cake with a very thin layer of frosting before adding more.

Pastry Bags:
Reusable 8", 12", and 18" bags should be plastic coated on the inside for easy cleaning. Clear plastic disposable bags are great for small jobs. However, these don't hold much frosting.

Coupling Nozzles:
Coupling nozzles are essential because they allow you to use your tips interchangeably. They can also act as a very large round writing tip for piping figures.

Pastry Tips:
Round writing tips are the most essential to the projects in this book. Leaf, star, and ribbon tips should also be in your repertoire. Try to have at least one from each of the following groups.
> Small round (#2, #3, #4)
> Medium round (#10 or #12)
> Large round (#5 or #6)
> Small star (#18 or #24)
> Medium star (#5)
> Large star (#4 or #8)
> Leaf (#66 or #67)
> Ribbon (#47 or #48)

Gel or Paste Food Coloring:
These are preferable to liquid food coloring because they are more concentrated and will not thin down the frosting.

Cake Boards or Foil-Covered Cardboard:

Party cakes take on odd shapes and large proportions. For this reason, they don't fit on standard cake platters. Cake decorating shops sell cake boards in a wide range of sizes. However, I find it most flexible to make my own. Simply cut the desired size from a sturdy cardboard box and cover with foil or baking parchment.

Waxed Paper:

Cut strips of waxed paper to slip underneath the edges of your unfrosted cake. When finished, you can pull them away and you won't have smeared the cake board.

Ice Cream Dreams

This is my favorite part of every party book . . . ICE CREAM. To me it's an edible art form that's as simple as sculpting with clay. You'll be amazed by the imaginative treats you can master in minutes . . . anything from coconut koala bears to an ice cream castle! There's no baking, no fuss, and no hot kitchen. It's so much fun to make ice cream creations that you can even turn it into a party activity. If you don't like to bake, buy the birthday cake and let the ice cream dessert become the party's focal point.

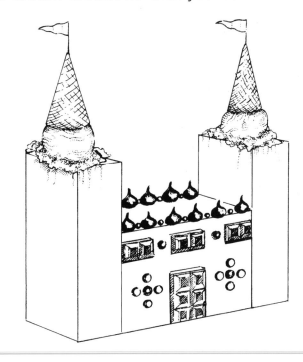

As with pastry tips, you'll notice that I refer to ice cream scoops by size. The food industry has assigned numbers for standardization. It's really not complicated, since you need only 2 for this book:

Large (#20 food scoop) makes about a $3^1/_2$ oz. serving
Small (#100 food scoop) makes about a $^1/_2$ oz. serving

These numbers may help you track down scoops in a kitchen shop, but what you want to remember is that a traditional scoop is large and a melon baller is small. Try to avoid self-defrosting scoops. These soften ice cream almost too fast while you're having to dish out a dozen peppermint-stick pink elephants! I prefer using the old-fashioned scoops with a release trigger on the side.

Working with ice cream can be as smooth as clockwork or like racing against a clock. It's simply a matter of planning ahead. Here are some tips I find helpful:

Always work with ice cream at the correct temperature. It should never be too soft or too hard to scoop.

Have all of your equipment set out ahead of time.

Have all of your garnishes ready and prepared (candies, raisins, cookies).

Have pastry bags prepared and filled with frosting for decorations.

Have one or more trays covered with aluminum foil. This will make ice cream creations easier to remove.

Keep any portion of ice cream that you're not working on in the freezer at all times.

Life's a Party!

Congratulations! You and your child are about to go on a big adventure, and I hope to be your guide for many years to come. Looking back, may you always remember those magical days filled with fantasy, food, and fun.

DINOSAUR DAY

AGES 3 TO 6

Generation after generation, the childhood infatuation with dinosaurs is rivaled only by that of Santa Claus. With each generation, it seems that more and more keep being discovered. Theories change, from what color they were to what brought about their extinction. But one thing remains constant . . . kids love dinosaurs. To some parents, it seems to border on obsession. Kindergartners can rattle off complex names that would tongue-tie an adult. Even though dinos only exist in encyclopedias and imaginations, kids have a very real relationship with these awesome creatures that once walked the earth. You can't miss by having a prehistoric party. It's a guaranteed hit for this age group. In fact, it's practically a rite of passage!

MENU

PTERODACTYL
WINGS

DINO DIP

T-REX CAKE

Party Elements

Invitation: Dinosaur Bone

Decorations: Paleontology Park signs, dinosaur tracks, crepe paper ferns, toy dinosaurs

Party Gear: Saber-toothed Tiger Headbands

Instant Involvement: Cave Painting

Games/Activities: Dizzy Dinosaurs, Boulder Buster, Fossil Hunt

Goody Bags: Jurassic Sacks

Invitation: Dinosaur Bone

Any paleontologist will tell you that finding a dinosaur bone is like discovering a buried treasure. That's why it's the perfect prelude to a prehistoric party. The invitation includes a suggestion sheet for cavepeople costumes. Of course, we all know that dinosaurs were long gone before the presence of humans. However, this popular anachronism has been with us since *The Flintstones.*

Materials:

1 20 x 30-inch sheet of beige poster board
pencil, scissors
brown felt-tip marker
12 computer printouts or photocopies of
    the COSTUME SUGGESTION SHEET
12 letter-size envelopes
dinosaur ink stamps and ink
Makes 12 invitations

Directions:

Make a paper pattern of a bone that will fit into envelopes (*Fig. 1*). Use this to cut out 12 bones from the poster board. With marker write:

Fig. 1

ANNOUNCING DINOSAUR DAY
AT PALEONTOLOGY PARK

On the reverse side of each bone, write:
   (your child's name) **CAVE AT**
       (your address)
    ON (date) **AT** (time) **RSVP**
       (your phone)

FOR EXTRA FUN
COME AS A CAVEMAN!

Fig. 2

Fold costume suggestion sheets (see below) around bones (*Fig. 2*) and slip into envelopes. Address envelopes and decorate with rubber stamps.

Costume Suggestion Sheet:

A caveperson's costume can be made out of anything that's fuzzy or looks like an animal skin print: a piece of fake fur, animal-print fabric or pajamas (leopard, tiger, or zebra), or even an old bathroom throw rug. No sewing is really necessary—cavemen didn't have sewing machines!

Bath Rug or Fur Cloth
Cut a neck hole in center of fabric, allowing enough fabric to fall down the front and back of your child to reach the knees. Drape around each side, trimming with scissors if necessary. Tie with a sash (*Fig. 3*).

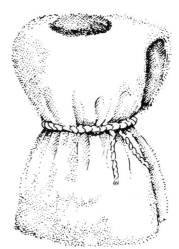

Fig. 3

Animal Print Fabric
Tie a piece of fabric, wide enough to drape around your child, in a knot over one shoulder. Tie costume in place at the waist with a sash or cord (*Fig. 4*).

Other Suggestions
Wear animal-print pajamas or decorate an old bathrobe or T-shirt to look like an animal skin.

NOTE: Cavepeople will want to wear swimsuits or leotards under costumes.

Fig. 4

 # Decorations

Creating the ambience for Dinosaur Day is easy if you just think in terms of a swamp. Greet guests arriving on the scene with signs like PALEONTOLOGY PARK and DO NOT FEED THE DINOSAURS

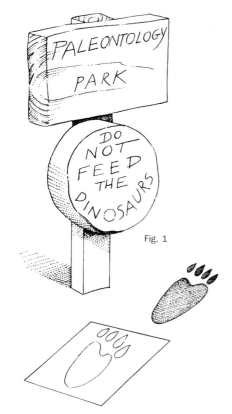

Fig. 1

(*Fig. 1*). Use sidewalk chalk or tempera paint to make dinosaur tracks up your driveway or front walk (*Fig. 2*). This setting calls for an abundance of ferns and plants. Cut long green fern leaves from green tissue paper and dangle them from green crepe paper streamers. Draw dinosaur silhouettes all over the tablecloth and paper plates and provide crayons for the kids to color them in (*Fig. 3*). Set the table with low-lying leafy plants, pebbles, and rocks. Select nice smooth stones, like the kind that you get from a garden center, to paint with each guest's name (*Fig. 4*). Use as place markers. Use plastic or stuffed toy dinosaurs around the table as part of the decor.

Fig. 2

Party Gear: Saber-Toothed Tiger Headbands

If you can't find tiger-print fake fur, just use orange or brown and color in stripes with a wide-tipped ink marker.

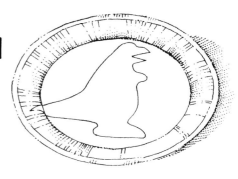

Fig. 3

Materials:
1 yard 48-inch to 60-inch-wide tiger-print
    fur cloth
tape measure
scissors
sewing machine or stapler
Makes 12 headbands

Fig. 4

Directions:

1. Use your child's head as a model.

2. Measure circumference of head and allow an extra $1^1/2$ inches.

3. Cut 12 strips of fabric from the cloth that are 4 inches wide and the length of the measurement.

4. Connect ends of fabric, right sides together, using $^3/4$-inch seams.

5. Sew or staple together (*Fig. 1*).

6. Reverse headband so that seam is on the inside (*Fig. 2*).

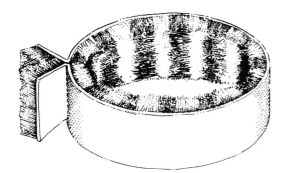

Fig. 1

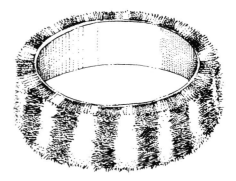

Fig. 2

Instant Involvement: Cave Painting

Art is always a great icebreaker and encourages kids to get into the Dinosaur Day spirit. As soon as the cavepeople start arriving, commission them to work on a cave painting. Tell the guests that they are creating a record of prehistoric life that will someday be discovered by a paleontologist and displayed in a museum. Since this mural is being painted on the wall of a "cave," choose a rec room, basement, or garage for the project. Tape wide rolls of brown wrapping paper completely around the area to be painted. Cover the floors with newspaper or drop cloths. Provide cans of colorful tempera paint and brushes. If you're nervous about having wet paint and children together in your house, you can also opt to do this with large crayons. After all the kids are present and the mural is reasonably complete, leave it up to dry and serve as a backdrop for the party.

Games/Activities

DIZZY DINOSAURS

This game is based on the same principle as "Upset the Fruit Basket." Instead of apples, oranges, strawberries, and pineapples, children are divided into groups of brontosauruses, stegosauruses, triceratops, and pterodactyls. Enough chairs are placed in a large circle (facing toward the center) to accommodate all but one child, who will play "it." The child who is "it" stands in the middle of the circle and announces his or her choice of dinosaur (from one of the four species). Example: If "it" calls out "triceretops," all of the triceratops must scramble to change their seats with one another. Meanwhile, "it" rushes to grab one of the empty seats. If "it" fails to get a seat, he or she remains "it" for the next turn. If "it" is able to get one of the seats, "it" becomes a triceratops, and the displaced dinosaur becomes "it."

BOULDER BUSTER

Think of this game as a form of prehistoric piñata. Cavepeople break paper-bag "boulders" with a baseball "club." Because these piñatas are so easy and inexpensive to make, you can have several so that every child gets a chance to take a swing. (This is the problem with a traditional piñata game using a single piñata: What happens if the first or second player in line breaks it? The other players feel left out.) To make boulders, stuff paper bags with shredded paper and candy. Crumple up bags until they're an irregular, rock shape. Tape sheets of gray tissue paper around bags so that they'll look like boulders. Tie packaging cord around each boulder, allowing a trail of cord long enough to hang over the limb of a tree and pull the bag up and down. (Indoors, you can use a hook or a pulley.) Have players line up behind the blindfolded "Boulder Buster." Give each player 3 to 5 swings at the boulder before moving on to the next in line. If the boulder breaks, the players in line rush in to gather up the candy. Keep hanging up boulders and letting players swing at them until everyone has had a chance or you run out of boulders.

FOSSIL HUNT

This is a variation on the classic Easter egg hunt, substituting dinosaur cookies (recipe follows) for eggs. The cookies are wrapped in plastic wrap or cellophane and hidden around the yard or in specific rooms in the house. Tell the guests that they are paleontologists, looking for "petrified dinosaurs." Have extra cookies waiting as a backup for kids who don't have much luck in finding things.

NOTE: This is a great recipe for old-fashioned brown sugar cookies. However, you can also roll out refrigerated cookie dough and cut with dinosaur-shaped cutters. If you're really pressed for time, just wrap clusters of dinosaur-shaped jelly candies in colored plastic wrap.

DINOSAUR COOKIES

Ingredients:
$1^1/_2$ cups (3 sticks) unsalted butter, softened
3 cups firmly packed brown sugar
1 tsp. vanilla extract
3 eggs
$4^1/_4$ cups all purpose flour
$1^1/_2$ tsp. baking soda
2 tsp. nutmeg
raisins or dried currants

Directions:
1. Cream butter, brown sugar, and vanilla together until light and fluffy.

2. Beat in eggs one at a time.

3. Stir flour, baking soda, and nutmeg together in a separate bowl.

4. Blend dry ingredients into butter mixture.

5. Wrap dough in plastic and chill at least 3 hours.

6. Preheat oven to 350°F (180°C).

7. Roll out dough on a floured surface and cut with dinosaur-shaped cookie cutters.

8. Place at least $1^1/_2$ inches apart on cookie sheets lined with baking parchment. (This makes the cookies easy to remove without breaking any legs, necks, or tails.)

9. Bake about 8 minutes until lightly golden in color.

10. Cool completely on parchment and gently lift off the paper with a spatula.

PHOTO OPS

Get kids to pose alongside their original cave paintings in their caveman costumes. Another cute shot for thank-you notes is to capture each child on film as they're blindfolded and swinging at boulders.

Goody Bags: Jurassic Sacks

Use rubber stamps of dinosaurs to decorate natural-colored tote bags. Fill with dinosaur-theme trinkets and toys. (There's an abundance out there, from pencil erasers to miniature coloring books.) Add dinosaur-shaped candies and chocolate eggs.

 # Recipes

PTERODACTYL WINGS

Although chicken wings can be disjointed into drummettes, these are left whole to resemble the wingspan of a pterodactyl.

Ingredients:

24 whole chicken wings
4 eggs
$2/3$ cup vegetable oil
2 Tbs. prepared barbecue sauce, plus extra for dipping
all-purpose flour
5 cups cornflake crumbs
Serves 12

Directions:

1. Preheat oven to 375°F (190°C).

2. Wash and dry chicken wings.

3. Stretch wings out so they look like they're ready to fly.

4. Beat eggs, oil, and barbecue sauce together.

5. Set out two shallow pans, one holding flour and the other with cornflake crumbs.

6. Dredge chicken wings lightly in flour.

7. Dip wings in egg mixture and coat with cornflake crumbs.

8. Cover a large baking sheet with foil, shiny side down, and coat with nonstick cooking spray.

9. Arrange wings on foil and bake for 20 minutes.

10. Turn wings carefully so as not to break the crust.

11. Bake 20 minutes longer, or until golden brown. Serve with additional barbecue sauce.

DINO DIP

Even self-proclaimed vegetable haters will dig into this "dippy dinosaur." Of course, you can also add potato chips.

Ingredients:
large acorn squash
4 long, narrow, curved zucchini
2 whole cloves
bamboo skewers or sturdy toothpicks
DINO DIP (recipe follows)
DIPPERS: celery sticks, carrot sticks, zucchini slices, potato chips, and/or pretzel rods
Serves 12

Directions:

1. Split acorn squash in half lengthwise. From 2 of the zucchini, cut off 2-inch pieces from the ends, giving you 4 "legs." (Slice up the zucchini left in the midsection for dippers.)

2. Use toothpicks to attach legs to squash (*Fig. 1*).

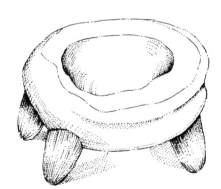

Fig. 1

3. For neck and head: Cut a gash in one of the remaining zucchini and fold down, forward, using a toothpick to secure in place. Insert cloves for eyes (*Fig. 2*).

4. Attach neck to one end of the squash with toothpicks and the remaining zucchini (to the other end) for the tail (*Fig. 3*).

5. Serve on a large platter with dip filling the center of the squash. Surround with dippers.

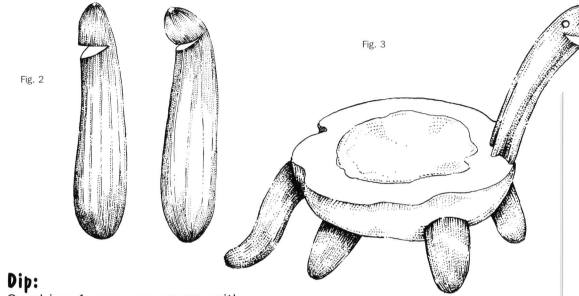

Fig. 2

Fig. 3

Dip:

Combine 1 cup sour cream with
$^1/_4$ cup mayonnaise
$^1/_3$ cup finely chopped seeded cucumber
2 Tbs. chopped dill pickle
and 1 Tbs. chopped fresh chives.

T-REX CAKE

Any sauropod will tell you that a tyrannosaurus is very intimidating, but you needn't feel intimidated by this T-rex cake. Make it from your child's favorite flavor of mix, or use the zucchini cake batter from the GREEN DRAGON CAKE RECIPE (pages 182–183). For that matter, you can use that recipe for GREEN CREAM CHEESE FROSTING, or simply tint canned vanilla frosting green...or purple (that is, if you want the cake the color of another very popular dinosaur!).

Ingredients:

9 x 13-inch baked sheet cake, cooled (use any flavor mix or zucchini cake from Green Dragon Cake, pages 182–183)
2 16-oz. cans vanilla frosting (or use Green Cream Cheese Frosting on pages 184–185)
green or purple paste or gel food coloring (if using canned frosting)
1 raisin
slivered almonds
Makes 12 servings

Directions:

1. Cover a 16 x 20-inch board with aluminum foil.

2. Cut cake according to diagram (*Fig. 1*).

3. Arrange cake pieces as shown on board (*Fig. 2*).

4. If using canned frosting, tint desired shade, or follow directions for Green Cream Cheese Frosting.

5. Frost cake with a smooth, even layer of frosting.

6. Use raisin for eye and slivered almonds for teeth and claws (*Fig. 3*).

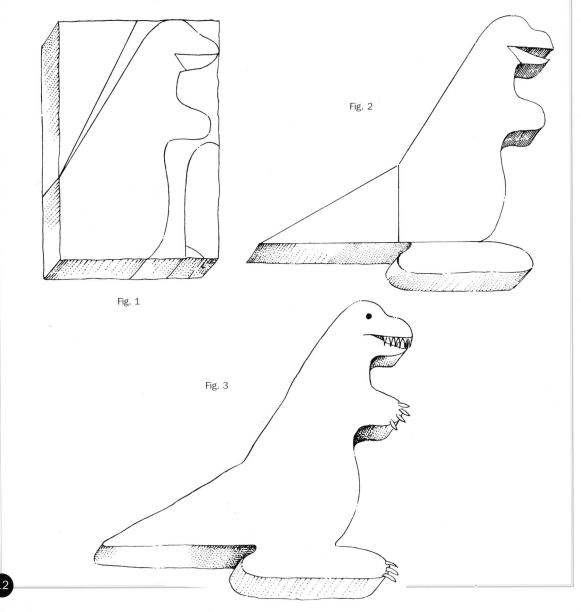

Fig. 1

Fig. 2

Fig. 3

Dino Dip (recipe pages 10–11)

Bear Cub Club Burgers on Teddy Bread
Buns (recipe pages 22–23)

PICNIC TIME FOR TEDDY BEARS

Up to age 4

●

Everyone remembers their first teddy bear. He was more than just a stuffed animal—he was an endearing and enduring lifetime friend. Chances are he's still around, somewhere, snuggled away in a very secure and special place. This party celebrates that early and special bond between a child and his or her teddy bear. Kids are invited to escort their teddies to a picnic at the Bear Cub Club for an afternoon of fun food and games. According to the age group, you can be very flexible with the theme. For example, 2 year olds may be old enough to interact with other children but will be frustrated by organized games. It's best to simply let them enjoy one another's company and the festive atmosphere. Three and 4 year olds will appreciate planned activities and feel less dependent on the presence of Mom or Dad for reinforcement.

MENU

BEAR CUB CLUB
BURGERS on TEDDY
BREAD BUNS

TEDDY TATER CHIPS

carrots and celery
sticks

BUTTERSCOTCH BEAR
CAKE

POLAR TEDDIES

HONEYBEE TEA

 Party Elements

Invitation: Bear Cub Club membership patch

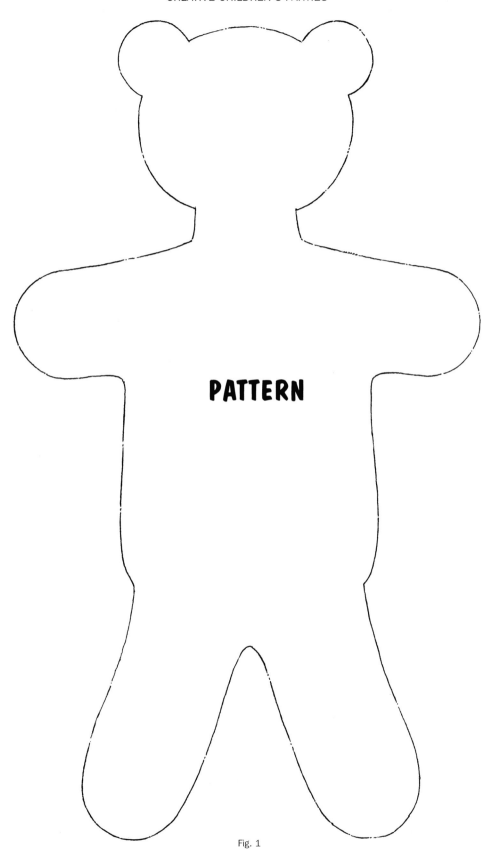

PATTERN

Fig. 1

Decorations: Trail of teddy bear signs, Bear Cub Club entrance, chains of "paper doll" bears, teddy bear balloons, Bear Cub Club plates and cups, edible play-dough bears.

Party Gear: Bear Cub Club Hats

Instant Involvement: "Best-Dressed Bear"

Games/Activities: Teddy Bear Toss, Teddy Bear Tag, or Musical Bears

Goody Bags: Bear Cub Club bags

 # Invitation: Membership Patch

This invitation includes a felt membership patch to the "Bear Cub Club." Mom can whipstitch or pin it onto a T-shirt or jacket.

Materials:
6 9 x 12-inch sheets of brown construction paper
6 9 x 12-inch squares of brown felt paper for pattern
pencil, pins, scissors
puff paint for fabric in writing tube (pink or
    light blue makes a nice contrast against
    the brown felt)
12 photocopies of invitation on pink or blue
    copier paper
paste or glue
7 x 9-inch envelopes
Makes 12 cards and patches

Directions:

1. Use pattern to cut 12 bears out of construction paper and 12 bears out of felt (*Fig. 1*).

2. With laundry marker, draw faces on felt bears and paper bears (*Fig. 2*).

3. Use puff paint to carefully write The Bear Cub Club across the body (*Fig. 3*).

4. Follow the manufacturer's directions for ironing patches (paint will puff up and feel fuzzy).

5. Trace around bear pattern on a plain sheet of copier paper.

Fig. 2

Fig. 3

THE
BEAR
CUB
CLUB

6. Write the following invitation as shown so that it fits into the outline:

PICNIC TIME FOR TEDDY BEARS!

Please bring your teddy for a party at
The Bear Cub Club
(address)
on (date) at (time)
RSVP (your phone number)

7. Make 12 copies on colored copier paper.

8. Cut out and paste to the back of the construction paper bear. Include a bear patch along with the invitation in each envelope.

 # Decorations

Guests will delight in following a trail of teddy bear road signs to your party. Make cardboard bears pointing the direction to your house along the route (*Fig. 1*).

THIS WAY

Fig. 1

Fig. 2

Fig. 3

Mount them on trees, telephone poles, or their own signposts (Note: Do not put up on traffic or public signs, or on private property without first obtaining permission.) Hang a Bear Cub Club *Members Only* sign on the front door and have a large stuffed teddy bear for the "doorman" (*Fig. 2*). You can make teddy bear balloons by gently painting inflated balloons with a quick-drying tempera paint (*Fig. 3*). Never overinflate balloons when painting them, or they'll pop from the slightest pressure. On the other hand, you'll want to paint them early in the morning or overnight so that they won't wither. In addition to the standard crepe paper streamers, add long chains of teddy bears cut from brown wrapping paper, "paper-doll" style (*Fig. 4*). Decorate the party table with a checkered tablecloth and a picnic basket with teddy bears sitting in it. Use a cookie cutter or pattern to draw outlines of teddy bears on plain paper place mats. Provide kids with boxes of crayons to fill in the bears and keep busy. Decorate plates and cups with the Bear Cub Club logo (*Fig. 5*). Shape edible play-dough into individual teddy bears for each child, using raisins for eyes and nose. Put one at each child's place setting, along with a name card (*Fig. 6*). Kids will have fun eating, mashing, smashing, or remodeling the dough.

Fig. 4

Fig. 5

Fig. 6

EDIBLE PLAY-DOUGH

Ingredients:

2 cups all-purpose flour
4 cups rolled oats
1 cup water
1 cup white corn syrup
1 cup peanut butter
$1^1/_4$ cups nonfat powdered milk
$1^1/_4$ cups powdered sugar

Directions:

1. Combine flour and oats in a food processor and pulverize oatmeal.

2. Add remaining ingredients and process until mixture is smooth. You may need to blend in more flour until mixture has a doughy consistency.

 # Party Gear: Bear Cub Club Ears

These simple hatbands let kids pretend that they're teddy bears too. For a custom fit, wait till the kids arrive and staple bands at the back.

Materials:

3 20 x 30-inch sheets of
    brown poster board
yardstick, pencil, scissors
pink or blue acrylic paint
    and brush
staples
Makes 12 party hats

PATTERN

Fig. 1

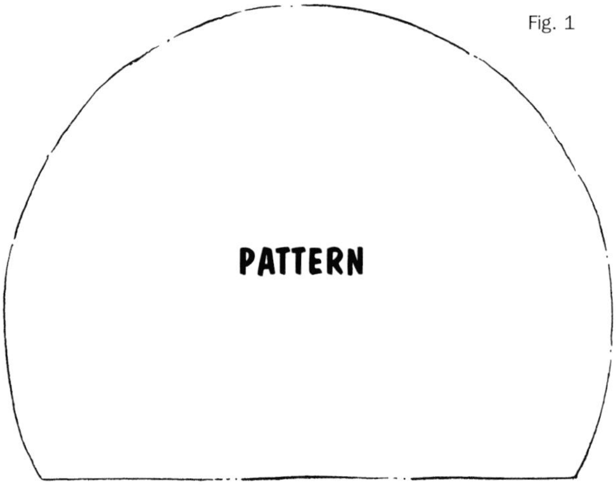

Directions:

1. Use yardstick to measure
    one sheet of poster board
    into 2 x 20-inch strips.

2. Cut ears according to pattern from the remaining sheets of poster
    board (*Fig. 1*).

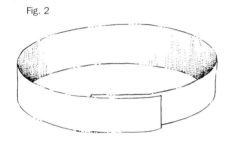

Fig. 2

3. Using your own child's head as a size
    guide, position band around head
    with ends overlapping at back (*Fig. 2*).

4. Mark the correct placement for ears
    with a pencil.

5. Staple ears to inside of the band
    (*Fig. 3*).

6. Paint BEAR CUB CLUB across
    front of bands (you can paint
    the child's name, instead).

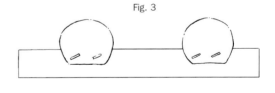

Fig. 3

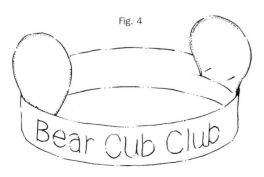

Fig. 4

7. Staple bands together in back
    after fitting on children's heads
    (*Fig. 4*).

19

Instant Involvement: "Best-Dressed Bear"

This is an engaging activity for children that helps set the tone for the rest of the party. Kids get to interact with each other through their teddy bears, which is a real icebreaker for those children who have never met. Make up a wardrobe box (or better yet, use a trunk or chest, if you have one). Inside the wardrobe, put all kinds of doll clothes, baby clothes, infant shirts, scarves, hats, sunglasses. . . . Let kids experiment with dressing up their teddy bears. Remember that teddy bears come in different sizes, so you'll need garments that will work for a variety of stuffed animal physiques. You can always borrow clothes from friends, neighbors, and the parents of party guests.

Games/Activities

TEDDY BEAR BOSS

In this spin on the traditional "Simon Says" game, children are interactive with their teddy bears. Kids line up facing the "Teddy Bear Boss." Everyone, including the boss, has his or her bear. The Teddy Bear Boss directs the other players to do some activity with their bear, such as swinging it by the feet, hugging it, waving its arm. Of course, the Teddy Bear Boss has to do and say whatever that action is before the other players can follow through. If the Teddy Bear Boss just performs an action (like kissing his or her Teddy Bear) without first saying it, and another child follows through, they have to form a new line behind the original one. (Obviously, if several kids are "out" they form the new line together.) The last player left in the front line becomes the next Teddy Bear Boss. The original principle of "Simon Says" has "out" players sit down or get pulled from the line. For this age group, it's more fun to keep everybody active in an "out line."

TEDDY BEAR TAG

Kids carry their teddy bears "piggyback" as they run away from one child who is designated as "it." If "it" tags another child's teddy bear, they must swap bears and the tagged child becomes "it." The game progresses like this until every child is carrying someone else's teddy bear, or it wears out—whichever happens first.

MUSICAL BEARS

In this noncompetitive version of musical chairs, kids scramble to seat their teddy bears in the available chairs. The difference between this and the classic game is: Teddy bears sit in the chairs instead of children, and instead of having "out" players standing around idly as each chair is removed, more teddy bears keep getting piled up in the same chair. Place chairs in a circle, facing outward, with one less chair than the number of teddy bears. Play an appropriate bear song like "Picnic Time for Teddy Bears." When the music stops, one chair is removed; the last chair to be filled must accommodate all of the remaining teddy bears. This continues as one chair is removed with each round until all of the kids are piling their bears into the same chair.

PHOTO OPS

Pose each child with his or her best-dressed bear for a memorable thank-you note snapshot. They'll make great family album photos for parents.

Goody Bags: Bear Cub Club Bags

Decorate small shopping bags with the Bear Cub Club logo. Add cellophane bags filled with gumdrop bears, cracker bears, and cookie bears. Include a collectible beanbag bear and perhaps a few chocolate teddy bears, miniature teddy bear puzzles, or coloring books with crayons.

 **Recipes**

BEAR CUB CLUB BURGERS ON TEDDY BREAD BUNS

Delightful teddy bear buns make these hamburgers almost too cute to eat. They're simple to make because you start with the convenience of frozen bread dough.

Ingredients:

2 lbs. ground beef
$1/3$ cup finely chopped onion
$1/2$ cup finely chopped red bell pepper
2 Tbs. ketchup
1 Tbs. Worcestershire sauce
$1/2$ tsp. salt
$1/4$ tsp. pepper
pickles, lettuce, and condiments
TEDDY BREAD BUNS (recipe follows)
Serves 12

Directions:

1. Combine ground beef, onion, red bell pepper, ketchup, Worcestershire sauce, salt, and pepper in a mixing bowl.

2. Shape into 12 3-oz. patties.

3. Broil or grill until hamburgers are fully cooked and juices run clear.

4. Slice open teddy bear buns and fill with patties.

5. Save plastic honey bear bottles and use them to serve ketchup and mustard.

TEDDY BREAD BUNS

Ingredients:

2 1-lb. loaves frozen bread dough
raisins
1 beaten egg

Directions:

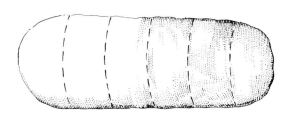

1. Defrost bread overnight in the refrigerator.

2. Divide each loaf into 6 equal-size balls (*Fig. 1*).

Fig. 1

3. Divide each ball into 1 large and 3 small balls (*Fig. 2*).

4. Flatten large ball and press 2 small balls into the top for ears, and 1 onto the face for a nose (*Fig. 3*).

5. Push raisins into dough for nose and eyes (*Fig. 4*).

6. Cover with plastic wrap and let rise in a warm place until doubled in bulk.

Fig. 2

Fig. 3

Fig. 4

7. Preheat oven to 375°F (190°C) and bake 20 to 30 minutes or until golden brown (*Fig. 5*).

Fig. 5

TEDDY TATER CHIPS

Large bag of your favorite brand of potato chips—enough for 12 small servings.

BUTTERSCOTCH BEAR CAKE

Old-fashioned brown sugar penuche frosting makes this cake a lick-the-spoon treat. However, if you want a quicker frosting that's also a suitable "bear shade of beige," try the peanut butter frosting.

Ingredients:

2 cups all-purpose flour
2 cups firmly packed dark brown sugar
$1/2$ cup butter-flavored shortening
1 cup buttermilk
1 tsp. baking soda
$3/4$ tsp. vanilla
3 eggs
1 small donut
1 large black gumdrop
2 small black gumdrops
Serves 12

Directions:

1. Preheat oven to 350°F (180°C). Line a 9 x 13-inch pan with baking parchment.

2. Combine flour, sugar, shortening, buttermilk, baking soda, vanilla, and eggs in a large mixing bowl.

3. Beat on medium speed for about 30 seconds, scraping bowl with spatula.

4. Beat on high speed for 3 minutes, scraping bowl occasionally.

5. Pour into pan and bake 40 to 45 minutes.

6. Cool cake 10 minutes.

7. Remove cake from pan and cool completely.

8. Cut cake as shown (*Fig. 1*).

9. Cover a 15 x 17-inch board with foil.

10. Arrange pieces of cake as shown (*Fig. 2*).

11. Use some frosting to position donut on face (*Fig. 3*).

12. Cover with frosting and use large gumdrop for nose and small gumdrops for eyes.

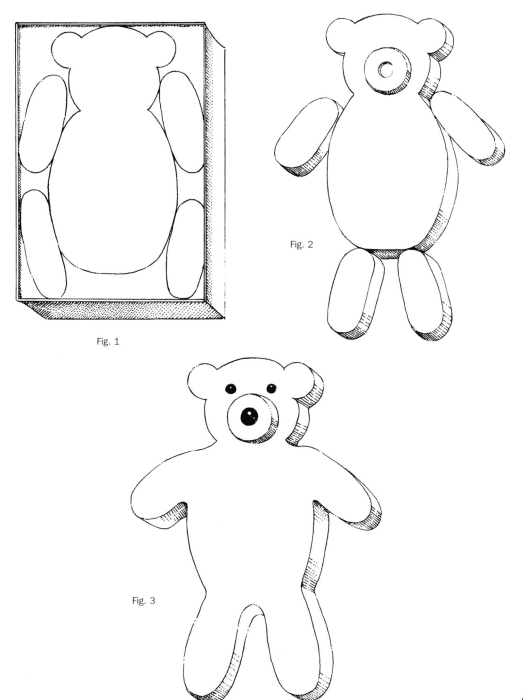

Fig. 1

Fig. 2

Fig. 3

BROWN SUGAR PENUCHE FROSTING

Ingredients:

$1/2$ cup butter or margarine
1 cup firmly packed brown sugar
$1/4$ cup milk
2 cups powdered sugar

Directions:

1. Melt butter in a 2-quart saucepan.

2. Stir in brown sugar.

3. Heat to boiling, stirring constantly.

4. Remove from heat and cool to lukewarm.

5. Place pan over bowl of cold water.

6. Beat until frosting is smooth and of spreading consistency. If frosting becomes too stiff, beat in additional milk, 1 tsp. at a time.

PEANUT BUTTER FROSTING

Ingredients:

$1/4$ cup (1/2 stick) butter or margarine, softened
$1/2$ cup creamy peanut butter
1 teaspoon vanilla extract
$4^{1}/2$ cups (1 pound) confectioner's sugar
5–7 tablespoons milk

Directions:

1. Combine butter, peanut butter, and vanilla extract in a large mixing bowl.

2. Beat with electric mixer until smooth.

3. Blend in confectioner's sugar.

4. Beat in enough milk to make frosting smooth and of spreading consistency.

POLAR TEDDIES

Coconut snowballs are a dessert classic. This takes the idea one step further and turns them into teddy bears—polar teddy bears!

Ingredients:

1 gallon vanilla ice cream
2 cups flaked coconut
12 large marshmallows
1 4-oz. can chocolate fudge
    frosting
large ice cream scoop (#20 food scoop)
small ice cream scoop (#100 food scoop)
pastry bag with coupling nozzle and #2
    or #4 round writing tip
Serves 12

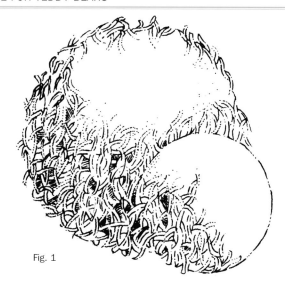

Fig. 1

Fig. 2

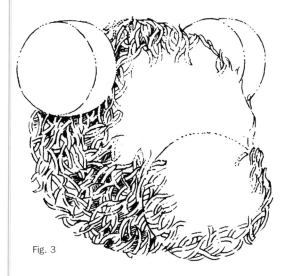

Fig. 3

Directions:

1. Cover a tray with aluminum foil. Put coconut in a pie pan (it's easier to use half of it at one time).

2. Working quickly, roll a large scoop of ice cream in coconut and place on foil.

3. Roll a small scoop in coconut and press against large scoop (*Fig. 1*). If ice cream gets too soft at any time, return to freezer.

4. Cut each marshmallow in half, into round "ears" (*Fig. 2*). Attach ears to bear heads, using toothpicks (*Fig. 3*).

5. Fill pastry bag with frosting and use to pipe nose, eyes, and eyebrows (*Fig. 4*).

6. Return to freezer at least 3 hours before serving.

Fig. 4

HONEYBEE TEA

Honeybee tea is the all-time favorite beverage of teddy bears.

Ingredients:

1 quart apple juice
1 quart pineapple juice
$1/2$ gallon iced tea
$1/2$ cup honey
Makes 1 gallon

Directions:

Combine ingredients in a large punchbowl or plastic bottle. Chill until serving time or pour over ice. For fun, you can serve the beverage from teapots on the table.

PINK ELEPHANT CIRCUS PARTY

AGES 4 TO 6

A ny child is likely to tell you that the circus is one of the most magical experiences on earth. Whether it's under the traditional "big top" or in a metropolitan coliseum, every child remembers his or her first circus just as vividly as if it happened yesterday. For example, I was terrified of clowns. On the other hand, I was enchanted with the tightrope, trapeze, trained tigers . . . and Technicolor elephants! I knew all of these animals were from exotic lands, but what I really wanted to know was where those "pink pachyderms" came from. Looking back, I guess they'd been painted with some kind of tempera paint. I'll always associate the circus with these fantasy creatures, which are the inspiration for this fun twist on a classic theme party.

Party Elements

Invitation: Peanut Bag

Decorations: Circus signs, elephant footprints, sideshow animal attractions, big top tent, circus posters, pink elephant balloons, pink elephant play clay

Party Gear: Pink Elephant Ears and Trunks

MENU

BIG TOP JUMBO BURGER

PAPRIKA PINK RINGMASTER FRIES

ORANGE ELEPHANTS

PINK ELEPHANT CAKES

PEPPERMINT ICE CREAM PACHYDERMS

PINK ELEPHANT PUNCH

Instant Involvement: Circus Wagon Workshop

Games/Activities: P. T. Barnum Says, Tent Pitching, Pink Elephant Parade

Goody Bags: "Jumbo" Totes

Invitation: Peanut Bag

Hand-deliver these pink, peanut-packed sacks with tickets to the "Greatest Show on Earth." Party supply shops are a great resource for a rainbow selection of colored lunch bags. Make pink admission tickets on your computer, or use a copier machine.

Materials:

5 x 10-inch pink lunch sacks
red felt-tip marker
pink laser printer or copier paper
black marker, ruler, scissors
unshelled peanuts
pink ribbon
stapler
Makes 12 invitations

Directions:

1. On the outside of each lunch sack, write "Pink Elephant Peanut Bag." You can also draw an elephant head on the sack (*Fig. 1*).

Fig. 1

Fig. 2

2. Divide a sheet of paper so that you'll have 6 tickets, approximately 3 x 4 inches, using a ruler and marker.

3. On each ticket, write or print:

THE PINK ELEPHANT CIRCUS

ADMISSION TICKET: Admit one pink elephant
Under the Big Top (your address)
(date and time) **RSVP** (your phone number)

4. Make two printouts or photocopies of the tickets and cut apart.

5. Fill bags halfway up with peanuts and add one ticket to each bag.

6. Fold down the top of the bag and staple a ribbon in place, through all thicknesses.

7. Tie ribbon in a bow (*Fig. 2*).

Decorations

Some strategically placed signs at the end of your street or driveway, such as CIRCUS GROUNDS AHEAD or PINK ELEPHANT CROSSING (*Fig. 1*), will announce to your guests that they're on the right course. Use pink sidewalk chalk or tempera paint to make "elephant tracks" for guests to follow up your driveway or front walk (*Fig. 2*). Put up a banner across the garage or front door that says THE GREATEST SHOW ON EARTH! (*Fig. 3*). Inside the garage (or party room) you can put stuffed animals in sideshow attraction cages. Cut front openings in large boxes and string yarn across the opening for bars. Paint or decorate the boxes to look like "circus-style" cages. Around the

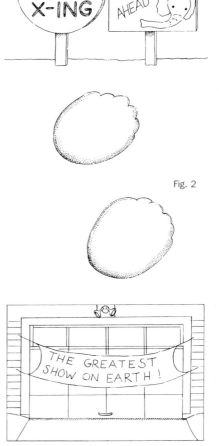

Fig. 1

Fig. 2

Fig. 3

party room, put up some circus posters, P. T. Barnum style. These could be cartoon-like drawings of gigantic pink elephants pitching tents or standing on their hind legs. Indoors or outdoors, you can create the effect of a "big top" tent. One way that works well indoors is to drape alternating rows of pink and white crepe paper streamers from a central point in the ceiling (a lighting fixture or fan) to edges around the wall. Outdoors, you can do the same treatment over a patio, or drape striped sheets across a clothesline (*Fig. 4*). Make pink elephant balloons by taping pink tissue paper ears and trunks to hanging balloons (*Fig. 5*). Of course, you'll want to set the table with either a pink or pink and white striped tablecloth, pink plates, cups, and napkins. For place markers, model pink play clay into the shapes of elephants and use trunks to hold place cards (*Fig. 6*). Kids can entertain themselves by scrunching up the clay and remodeling it into their own creations.

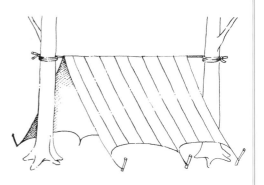

Fig. 4

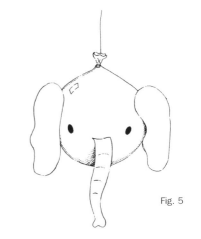

Fig. 5

Fig. 6

Party Gear: Pink Elephant Ears and Trunks

Playing "pretend pachyderm" really gets the party guests into the circus spirit. In addition to wearing elephant ears and trunks, you can also use face paint for a totally "pink" look.

Materials (ears):

1 20 x 30-inch sheet of pink poster
  board
3 20-inch x $2^1/_2$-yard packages of pink
  crepe paper
ruler, pencil, scissors
stapler
glitter paint in writing tube (red, blue, or
  green will contrast well)
Makes 12 ears

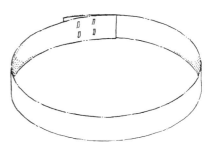

Fig. 1

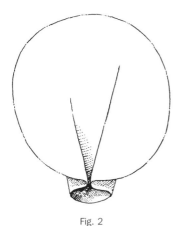

Fig. 2

Directions:

1. Cut the poster board into 12 2 x 20-
inch strips.

2. Staple the strips together to form
headbands, overlapping the ends
(*Fig. 1*). Use your child as a guide
for average head size.

3. Cut 24 12-inch diameter circles
from the crepe paper and make a
pinch pleat at the top of each
circle to form ears (*Fig. 2*).

4. Staple ears to the outside of each band and write a guest's name
on the front of each headband (*Fig. 3*).

Materials (trunks):

6 9 x 12-inch pieces of pink felt
12 pipe cleaners
pink thread, needle, scissors
sewing machine (optional)
12 mask bands or elastic cord
Makes 12 trunks

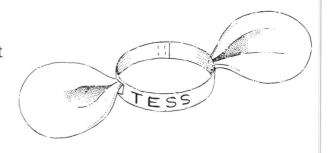

Fig. 3

Directions:

1. Cut felt into 9 x 6-inch sections.

2. For each trunk: Place a pipe cleaner along the length of one edge of
felt (*Fig. 4*).

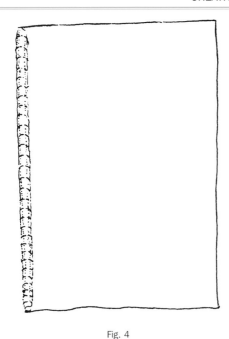

Fig. 4

3. Whipstitch pipe cleaner in place by hand (or zigzag on the sewing machine).

4. Make a tube out of the felt and whipstitch in place (*Fig. 5*).

5. Tack-stitch one end of trunk together in the middle (*Fig. 6*).

6. Stitch mask band (or cut elastic cord to lengths that will gently stretch around a child's head) to each side of the open end of the trunk.

7. Bend trunk as desired (*Fig. 7*).

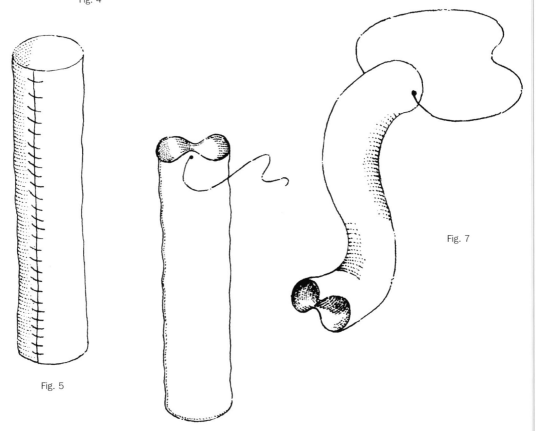

Fig. 5

Fig. 6

Fig. 7

Instant Involvement: Circus Wagon Workshop

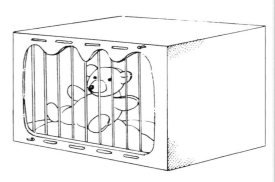

Fig. 1

This is one of those great get-acquainted activities that immediately bring party guests together for an exciting project. Kids create their own circus wagons and floats for a big "Pink Elephant Parade" at the end of the party. Plan on borrowing about 6 wagons, or 1 for every 2 party guests. Half of the wagons can be decorated like circus cages, and the other half can be decorated as floats, Rose Bowl style. For circus wagons: Cut out sides of boxes that will fit into wagons. String pieces of yarn across one side of the opening for bars. Let kids decorate the boxes with crayons or tempera paint (*Fig. 1*). Note: If using paint, allow some time for it to dry during the party before the grand finale parade. For floats: To create a flower effect, tear assorted colors of tissue paper into strips and wad up like carnations. Separate into baskets according to color. Let kids pick their colors and show them how to stick the tissue paper flowers to the sides of the wagon, using loops of tape. The crumpled tissue should be densely spaced so that you can't see any of the wagon sides. Wrap wagon pulls with crepe paper streamers and add trails of streamers down the sides (*Fig. 2*). Depending on the age of the party guests, you might want to get the wagons started and just let the kids do the finishing touches.

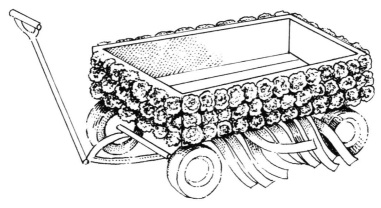

Fig. 2

Games/Activities

P. T. BARNUM SAYS

This game is a circus version of "Simon Says." The "pink elephants" form a large circle around one player, who starts off as "P. T. Barnum" and stands in the center. P. T. Barnum acts as ringmaster; the pink elephants get down on all fours and wait for performance commands. For example, P. T. could order the elephants to stand on the left leg, stand on the right leg, balance on their front legs (hands), turn in a small circle, walk around the ringmaster in a large circle, put their front legs on the back of the elephant next to them, flap their elephant ears, or make an elephant noise. Of course, none of these commands is valid unless P. T. says "RINGMASTER SAYS." The first elephant caught following a bogus order replaces P. T. Barnum in the center of the circle. You can be sure that most of the elephants will seem untrainable, just so they get a chance to be ringmaster.

TENT PITCHING

One marvel of my childhood was when my father took me to see an old-fashioned circus on the outskirts of town. At that time, the big shows were all in coliseums. He wanted me to experience the wonder and charm of the "big top." As we approached the circus grounds, I was awed by the elephants pitching tents. They were swinging mallets with their trunks and driving stakes into the ground. It was as if a scene from one of my storybooks had come to life.

This relay match turns the circus tradition of elephant labor into a game. Divide players into two teams. Make two rows of garden stakes, one for each player on each team. Each team gets a mallet or wooden hammer. Give a signal for the race to begin. The first elephant (player) on each team rushes up to that team's row of stakes and grabs the wooden mallet. The players pound their stakes into the ground and return to their team's line. Then the next player in line takes a turn driving in the next stake. This progression continues until the first team to drive all of the stakes into the ground wins.

PINK ELEPHANT PARADE

This is the grand finale and climax of the party. The wagons that were decorated when guests first arrived are now ready to roll. The circus wagon cages can be filled with stuffed animals (or live pink elephants). Pink elephants take turns pulling the wagons and riding in the floats. For musical accompaniment, pass out noisemakers such as party whistles, kazoos, cymbals, and oatmeal-carton drums. The parade route can go down the drive or sidewalk, with a reviewing stand at the end of the path.

PHOTO OPS

Take pictures of the kids while they're crafting parade floats in the circus wagon workshop. Later, you can photograph the herd of pink elephants as each one passes by the review stand. Enclose photos of party guests with, of course, pink thank-you notes.

Goody Bags: "Jumbo" Totes

Purchase pink tote bags from a party shop. Cut ears from pink construction paper and glue to the sides of the bags. Cut long strips of pink construction paper and fold back and forth, zigzag style. Glue to the front of bags for elephant trunks. Glue on hobby eyes or draw on eyes. Line bags with pink tissue paper or Easter grass, then fill bags with all kinds of pink stuff such as: bubblegum, jelly beans, fruit rolls, prepackaged cotton candy, popcorn balls wrapped in pink cellophane, and, of course, marshmallow

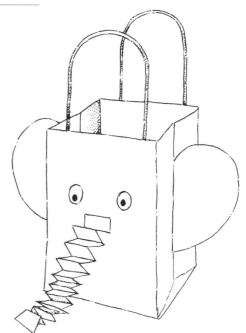

peanuts. Pink party favors might include yo-yos or whistles. Also look for circus-related toys like plastic animals or beanbag elephants.

 **Recipes**

BIG TOP JUMBO BURGER

Imagine a hamburger big enough to feed 12 hungry pink elephants! It's really a meatloaf baked in the shape of a giant hamburger patty on a jumbo bun. This mouthful becomes both the centerpiece and focal point of the party table. Simply slice in wedges and serve.

Ingredients:

2 eggs
1 cup milk
1 cup chili sauce or barbecue sauce
1 Tbs. Worcestershire sauce
1 tsp. salt
$1/2$ cup chopped onion
$1/2$ cup chopped celery
$1^1/2$ cups fresh bread crumbs
3 lbs. lean ground beef
JUMBO BUN (recipe follows)
mayonnaise (regular or reduced fat)
green-leaf or salad bowl lettuce
condiments: ketchup, mustard, dill pickle slices
Makes 12 servings

Directions:

1. Preheat oven to 350°F (180°C).

2. Beat eggs in a large mixing bowl.

3. Blend in milk, chili sauce, Worcestershire sauce, salt, onion, celery, and bread crumbs.

4. Mix in ground beef.

5. Line a 12-inch springform pan or a 13-inch deep-dish pizza pan with foil. Spray with nonstick cooking spray.

6. Press meat mixture into the prepared pan.

7. Bake for 1 to $1^1/4$ hours or until center of loaf is well done.

8. Drain off fat. Invert "burger" over a cookie sheet.

9. Remove from pan and peel off foil.

10. Split open bun with a long bread knife.

11. Spread the bottom of the bun with a layer of mayonnaise.

12. Arrange lettuce leaves on the mayonnaise and slide the burger on top.

13. Garnish the top of the burger with ketchup, mustard, and pickle slices (or serve plain and put the condiments on the table). Cover with top half of bun. Serve at the table and slice into wedges.

JUMBO BUN

Ingredients:
1 package rapid-rise active dry yeast
$1/4$ cup warm water
4 cups all-purpose flour
$1/4$ cup sugar
$1 1/2$ tsp. salt
$1/2$ cup hot water
$1/2$ cup milk
$1/4$ cup butter, softened
1 whole egg and 1 egg white
1 Tbs. sesame seeds

Directions:
1. Dissolve yeast in warm water in large bowl.

2. Mix in 2 cups of the flour.

3. Add sugar, salt, hot water, milk, butter, and whole egg until moistened.

4. Beat 2 minutes with electric mixer until smooth.

5. Stir in remaining 2 cups flour by hand.

6. Cover bowl with plastic wrap and let dough rise in warm place until doubled in size (about 30 minutes).

7. Punch dough down.

8. Turn out on a lightly floured board and knead until no longer sticky.

9. Grease a large baking sheet and sprinkle with cornmeal.

10. Trace an 11-inch circle on baking sheet (this can be done with a toothpick).

11. Form dough into a large ball, place on baking sheet, and pat evenly into a flattened 11-inch circle.

12. Lightly beat the egg white and brush on dough.

13. Let rise until doubled in bulk (30 to 35 minutes).

14. Preheat oven to 350°F (180°C).

15. Bake 30 to 40 minutes, or until the bun is golden brown and sounds hollow when tapped.

16. Cool. Use a bread knife to split open like a hamburger bun. As a shortcut, you can substitute a loaf of frozen bread dough.

PAPRIKA PINK RINGMASTER FRIES

Sprinkle 2 or 3 16-oz. bags of curly fries with paprika and bake according to directions.

ORANGE ELEPHANTS

These cute orange sculptures are nice table decorations to have waiting at each child's place setting.

Ingredients:
12 navel oranges
4 dozen large orange gumdrops (or use large crescent-shaped orange gumdrops, cut in half)
toothpicks
2 dozen whole cloves
Makes 12 elephants

Directions:

1. For each elephant: Hold orange so that the navel is facing down.

2. Make a V-shaped cut on one side of the orange for the tail (*Fig. 1*).

3. On the opposite side, make a Y-shaped cut for the trunk (*Fig. 2*).

4. Make C-shaped cuts for the ears (*Fig. 3*).

5. Gently pull all cut portions away from the orange, so that the tail, trunk, and ears stand out.

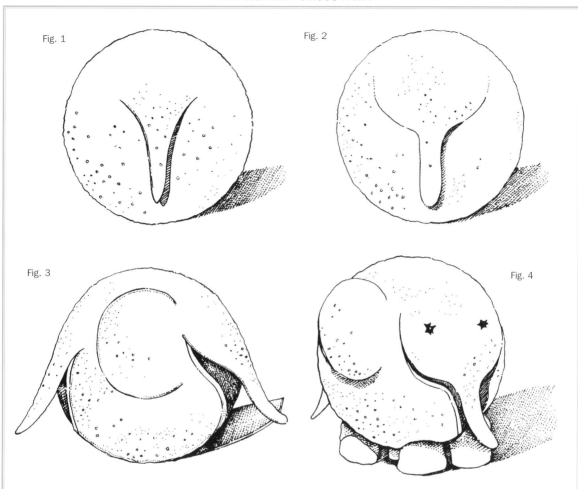

Fig. 1

Fig. 2

Fig. 3

Fig. 4

6. Insert 2 cloves for eyes.

7. Use toothpicks to anchor gumdrop legs in place (*Fig. 4*).

PINK ELEPHANT CAKES

My most memorable childhood birthday cake was a pink elephant. I actually saw some of these mythical creatures at a circus and was mesmerized by the vision. It was all I could talk about for months. Mom made my day when she came up with this cake creation. (As all mothers know, the annual party cake can become a major challenge. It's often based on a child's transient obsession. I've heard of requests for everything from grasshoppers to golf carts.)

This cherry-flecked batter can also be accomplished with a white cake mix. Simply add the chopped maraschino cherries to the batter and substitute $1/2$ cup of the cherry juice for the liquid in the package instructions. If you're really in a hurry, how about baking strawberry pink elephant cakes? Simply use strawberry cake mix and strawberry canned frosting.

Ingredients:

$2^1/4$ cups all purpose flour
$1^2/3$ cups sugar
$3^1/2$ tsp. baking powder
1 tsp. salt
$1/3$ cup shortening
$1/3$ cup butter, softened
$3/4$ cup milk
$1/2$ cup maraschino cherry juice
$1/2$ tsp. almond extract
5 egg whites
2 dozen stemmed maraschino cherries, chopped
CHERRY CREME FROSTING (recipe follows)
6 chocolate kiss candies
Makes 3 cakes

Directions:

1. Preheat oven to 350°F (180°C).

2. Line 3 8-inch round cake pans with baking parchment.

3. Combine flour, sugar, baking powder, and salt in a large mixing bowl.

4. Add shortening, butter, milk, cherry juice, and almond extract.

5. Beat for 2 minutes.

6. Add egg whites and beat for 2 minutes longer.

7. Fold in chopped cherries.

8. Divide batter among pans and bake 25 to 30 minutes, or until a toothpick inserted in the center comes out clean.

9. Cool cakes completely, invert from pans, and peel off parchment paper.

10. Use 3 14-inch round cake boards or platters. Each board will be used for one elephant cake. (I like to place one in the center of the table and one at each end—just like a three-ring circus.)

11. Cut cakes according to diagram (*Fig. 1*).

12. Arrange on boards according to diagram (*Fig. 2*).

13. Frost cakes with cherry frosting and use chocolate kisses for eyes (*Fig. 3*).

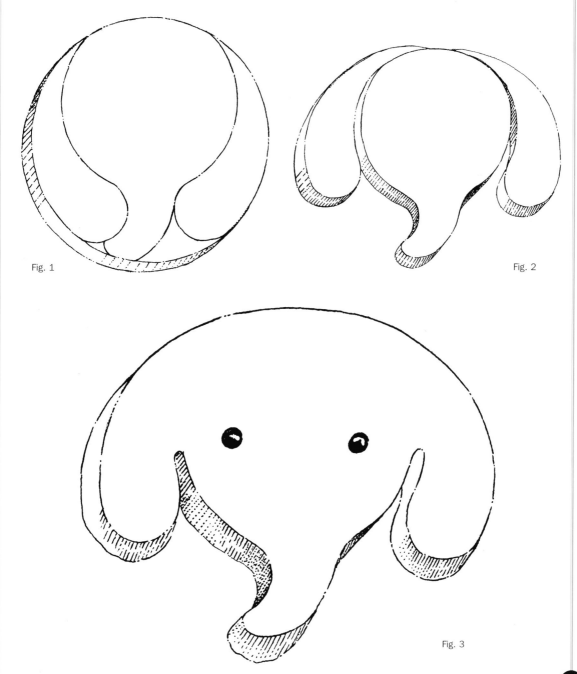

Fig. 1

Fig. 2

Fig. 3

CHERRY CREME FROSTING
Ingredients:
$1/2$ cup unsalted butter, softened
1 cup shortening
7 cups powdered sugar (about $1^{1}/2$ lbs.)
3 Tbs. maraschino cherry juice
3 (or more) Tbs. milk
1 tsp. almond extract
red gel or pink paste food coloring

Directions:

1. Cream butter and shortening in a mixing bowl until fluffy.

2. Add powdered sugar, cherry juice, milk, and almond extract.

3. Beat until smooth and creamy, adding an additional spoonful of milk if necessary.

4. Tint icing pink using either a few drops of red gel food coloring or some pink paste food coloring.

NOTE: Paste coloring is more intense than gel coloring.

PEPPERMINT ICE CREAM PACHYDERMS

Don't feel that you must limit yourself to peppermint ice cream for this party treat. Cherry or strawberry ice cream also works well. You can even use sorbet, as long as it's pink.

Ingredients:
PINK FONDANT (recipe follows)
$1/2$ gallon peppermint (or cherry or strawberry) ice cream
2 dozen chocolate chips
large ice cream scoop (#20 food scoop)
Serves 12

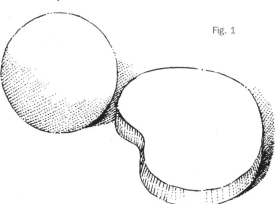

Fig. 1

Directions:

1. Shape fondant into 24 1-inch balls and 12 2-inch balls.

2. Flatten 1-inch balls into circles for elephant ears (*Fig. 1*).

Orange Elephants
(recipe pages 40–41)

Pirate Ship Pizzas
(recipe pages 55–56)

3. Shape 2-inch balls into elephant trunks (*Fig. 2*).

4. Cover a tray with aluminum foil.

5. Scoop 12 large round scoops of ice cream onto foil.

6. Press ears and trunks into ice cream scoops so that they resemble elephant heads.

7. Use chocolate chips for eyes (*Fig. 3*). Return to freezer until serving time.

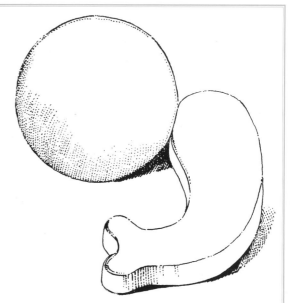

Fig. 2

Fig. 3

PINK FONDANT

Ingredients:

$1/3$ cup light corn syrup
$1/4$ cup unsalted butter, softened
1 tsp. peppermint extract (or almond extract, if using cherry or
    strawberry ice cream)
$4^3/4$ cups powdered sugar (about 1 lb.)
red gel or pink paste food coloring

Directions:

1. Combine corn syrup, butter, and peppermint extract in mixing bowl with 1 cup powdered sugar.

2. Blend until smooth.

3. Add remaining powdered sugar 1 cup at a time, blending with enough food coloring to make a pink candy dough.

PINK ELEPHANT PUNCH

Just about any pink drink will do, from Hawaiian punch to raspberry ginger ale. My favorite is to serve pink lemonade mixed with pureed frozen strawberries.

PIRATES PARTY

AGES 5 TO 8

Playing pirate has captured the imaginations of young boys for generations, making the theme a party classic. A gathering of "buccaneers," "swashbucklers," and assorted ruffians is usually regarded as a "boy thing." However, don't discount your daughter's interest in getting involved in the activities. As a little girl, one could say I had the "Peter Pan syndrome" too. After all, my brother was having so much fun! Our tree house was the crow's nest of our "shipwrecked schooner." The neighborhood girls wore pirate patches and defended the deck with mock sword fights, right along with the boys. So don't discount female siblings or friends as enthusiastic party guests.

MENU

PIRATE SHIP PIZZAS

TREASURE ISLAND
CHIPS AND DIP

SKULL AND CROSS-
BONES BROWNIES

ICE CREAM VOLCANO

GINGER BREW

 Party Elements

Invitation: Message in a Bottle

Decorations: Bermuda Triangle sign, fishnets, starfish, seashells, toy parrots, ship table, map mats, skull and cross-bones flags, balloons, plates, and cups

Party Gear: Buccaneer Hats

Instant Involvement: Wardrobe Department

Games/Activities: Sinking Ship, Treasure Hunt

Goody Bags: Pirates' Plunder Sacks

Invitation: Message in a Bottle

What else would you expect? An invitation to a pirates' plunder party is a message in a bottle! Of course, these invitations need to be hand-delivered. If necessary, you could ship some of them in small boxes of packing peanuts. Individual Perrier bottles make very authentic-looking vessels. You can even buy corks at cookware shops to plug up the openings.

Materials:

12 6^1/$_2$-oz. Perrier bottles
   (or other small bottles)
beige copier or computer
   printer paper
felt-tip marking pen
12 corks (optional)
Makes 12 invitations

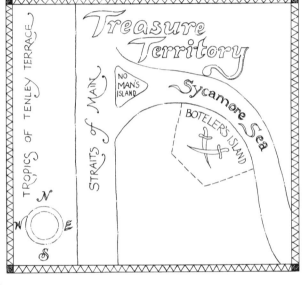

Directions:

The fun part of this invitation is creating a mythical map of your neighborhood. You can turn your street into a sea and your yard into an island. X marks the spot of your house on this treasure map. Keep in mind that this newly charted territory should bear a reasonable resemblance to the actual geography; you wouldn't want your guests to get lost

1. Draw up a map on the order of the example, applying the concept to your specific area.

2. On another sheet, write the following message:

Ship Ahoy and Shiver Me Timbers! They say there's a party of pirates at Captain (your child's name)**'s Hideaway. Calling all buccaneers, Barbary bandits, salty dogs, and sea scoundrels for great grub, games, and gold . . .** (date, time, your address) **RSVP** (your phone number) **Wear an oversize white shirt, rolled-up dark pants, and knee socks— the "Wardrobe Department" will take care of the rest!**

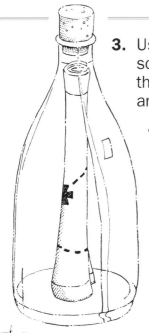

3. Using a photocopying machine or a computer scanner, run off copies on beige paper so that the map is on one side of each sheet and the invitation is on the other.

4. Distress or tear paper around the edges.

5. Fold in half lengthwise, and then roll up.

6. Soak bottles in water overnight and peel off labels.

7. Let bottles drain until thoroughly dry.

8. Put invitations in bottles and cork ends.

Fig. 1

 Decorations

From pirate ships of the past to jet planes of the present, legend has it that things seem to mysteriously disappear in the Bermuda Triangle. Why not direct your guests to the party by putting up an "ENTERING THE BERMUDA TRIANGLE" street sign (*Fig. 1*)? Other signs might be based on your child's name. For example, way back when my brother had a pirate party,

— we used sidewalk chalk to draw crossed palm trees on the driveway;

— then we wrote "BOTELER'S ISLAND" and "X MARKS THE SPOT" (*Fig. 2*).

— we draped a fishnet on the door, and

— put up a weathered sign that said "CAPTAIN BILLY'S HIDEAWAY," (*Fig. 3*).

Fig. 2

Fig. 3

When setting the party table up indoors,

— cover the table with a grass mat, fishnets, seashells, starfish, coconuts, pineapples, and other tropical fruits; if you make the Treasure Island Dip, it's a wonderful centerpiece.

For an outdoor party table, a whimsical treatment is to

1. Rig up sails down the middle of a picnic bench, using dowels, sheets, and clothesline (*Fig. 4*).

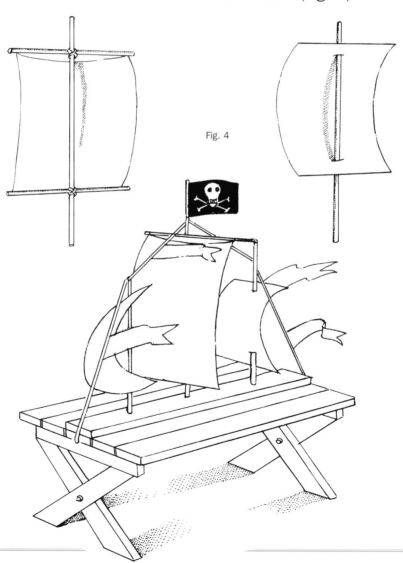

Fig. 4

2. Duplicate the map that you used for the invitation on plastic mats by drawing it with a laundry marker.

3. Provide the pirates with individual packs of crayons to color in the lines.

4. Use black plates and cups decorated with white skull and crossbones.

5. Blow up black balloons and use white paint for skull and crossbones (*Fig. 5*). Hang these from the ceiling or trees.

Fig. 5

 # Party Gear: Buccaneer Hats

These are some of the easiest party hats you'll ever make. Remember the classic paper hats that you used to fold out of newspaper? Well, these are the same principle. Black tissue paper, bright marabou plumes, and gold seal medallions will make you feel like a milliner for an MGM movie.

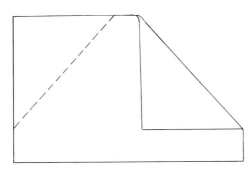

Fig. 1

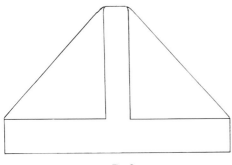

Fig. 2

Materials:

12 sheets of 20 x 30-inch black tissue paper
package of brightly colored craft feathers
12 gold pressure-sensitive medallion seals (available at stationery or office stores)
stapler
Makes 12 hats

Directions:

1. For each hat, fold a sheet of tissue into a 20 x 15-inch rectangle.

2. Fold again into a 10 x 15-inch rectangle, with the major fold at the top (*Fig. 1*).

3. Fold top corners down 7 inches and crease (*Fig. 2*). There should be a 1-inch space at the top (*Fig. 2*).

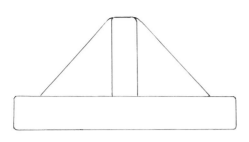

Fig. 3

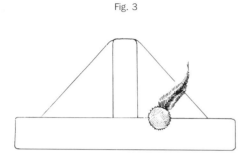

Fig. 4

4. Fold bottom edge, on each side, up by 1^1/$_2$ inches and staple hat together at edges (*Fig. 3*).

5. On the front of the hat, slightly off center, staple a feather behind the cuff.

6. Stick a gold medallion seal over the stapled end of the feather (*Fig. 4*).

 # Instant Involvement: Wardrobe Department

If your guests followed the instructions on the invitations, they should be arriving in partial garb: an oversize white shirt, rolled-up dark pants, and knee socks. Greet them at the door and escort them to the "Wardrobe Department." This can be any room designated with a sign above the door. Pretend that you're casting for "Treasure Island," the "Pirates of Penzance," or "Peter Pan." It's really up to the kids . . . after all, this party is a totally original production! Pass out the buccaneer hats, along with accessories such as eye patches, golden earrings, and sashes. A "makeup artist" can be on hand to apply mustaches with eyebrow pencil and scars with lipstick. As soon as a child is in costume, he or she can proceed to the crow's nest. This can be any window at a vantage point to view the arrival of other guests. A pair of binoculars or a small telescope adds an aura of excitement. It's the role of the pirates in the crow's nest to announce all newcomers by calling out their names, such as "Charlie ahoy!" If any pirates missed making their grand entrance (because they were early and no one was in the crow's nest), they can go outside and enter all over again.

Games/Activities

SINKING SHIP

For this game, you'll need to round up a couple of large appliance boxes. Lay boxes on their side and cut off the top so that several kids will be able to sit inside. Decorate boxes with crayons, markers, or tempera paint to resemble pirate ships. Position ships at opposite ends of the room, or about 12 to 16 feet apart if playing outdoors. Divide kids into two "crews." Each crew gets into the ship and may stand, sit, or kneel in it. The object of the game is to sink the opponents' ship with "cannon" (Ping-Pong) balls. Each ship is given one cannonball per player. At a signal, the ships begin "firing" (throwing) cannonballs at each other. The object is to land the cannonballs inside the opposing ship.

Cannonballs caught in midair may be thrown back at the other ship, but balls that land inside (on the deck) cannot be touched. Balls that fall outside the ship are "lost in the ocean." When there are no longer any balls left to throw, the ship with the most balls inside sinks, and the other ship is the victor. This game goes so fast that the kids will want to play several rounds.

TREASURE HUNT

A treasure chest filled with chocolate coins is truly a prize for any pirate. This game follows a series of clues that lead to the legendary "X" that marks the spot. You should gear your clues to the age group; the older the guests, the greater the challenge. A game that gives hints in riddle form will last longer than one in which the clues are quite obvious. Make the chest out of a shoe box covered with brown construction paper, and use gold or silver foil for straps or bands. Fill the box with bags of foil-wrapped chocolate coins (enough for everyone at the party).

Pretend that this treasure territory is somewhere in the tropics. It's best played outdoors but can also be played inside, as long as you have plenty of hiding places. Make up a total of 12 clues, 11 of them written on pieces of paper. The first clue is given to the crew of pirates by the "Ancient Mariner" (any adult present at the party). This could be something like: "Where the sea stands above the land," leading the players to a birdbath. A second clue might read: "Landlocked by a wooden wall," leading the players to a fence where the next clue might be wedged in the latch of a gate. (Of course, these are just examples. The clues you create will have to apply to your specific setting.) Players must not remove the clue from the spot where they find it, so that it can still be found by players coming along after them. The final clue will be a little map that shows the "Treasure Territory," with an "X" on the spot where the treasure chest is. As soon as a player finds the chest, he or she can take out one coin bag. However, the child has to put the chest back as he or she found it for the next player to find.

PHOTO OPS

Take pictures of pirates in the Wardrobe Department as they're getting into gear. Take photos of crews in their sinking ships for a great group shot.

Goody Bags: Pirates' Plunder Sacks

Sew muslin bags with drawstrings, or simply tie cord around a square of muslin (hobo bag style). You can also write "Captain (your child's name)'s Stash" on the front with a fabric marker or paint. Fill bags with all sorts of pirate party loot. Of course, you'll want to throw in the bags of classic chocolate coins. trail mix with dried pineapple and coconut, banana chips, and maybe a fresh orange. For favors, look for miniature toy telescopes, ships, toy stuffed parrots (or even colorful craft feathers), photocopies of treasure maps, or maps of the Caribbean along with crayons or markers for coloring in the lines.

Recipes

PIRATE SHIP PIZZAS

This simple party entree transforms hero rolls into schooner-shaped pizzas with paper pirate ship sails to take home as souvenirs.

Ingredients:

6 hero rolls, about 8 inches long
olive oil
1 16-oz. can pizza sauce
$1/4$ cup grated Parmesan cheese
2 cups shredded mozzarella cheese
$1 1/2$ cups chopped red and green bell pepper
16 oz. sliced pepperoni
PIRATE SAILS AND CROW'S NESTS (instructions follow)
Makes 12 servings

Directions:

1. Preheat oven to 350°F (180°C).

2. Split rolls in half lengthwise and lightly brush the cut surfaces with olive oil.

3. Stir Parmesan cheese into the pizza sauce and spread 2 or 3 tablespoons of sauce over the top of each roll.

4. Cover sauce with mozzarella cheese, chopped bell pepper, and pepperoni slices.

5. Bake 16 to 22 minutes, or until cheese is bubbling hot and melted.

6. Insert sails in center of pizzas and serve immediately.

NOTE: You can assemble these the day before, cover with plastic wrap, and bake just before serving.

PIRATE SAILS AND CROW'S NESTS

Cut sails from construction paper. They should be about 6 inches high and 4 inches wide at the base, tapering to 3 inches at the top. Use paint to make a skull and crossbones (*Fig. 1*). Insert a 9-inch wooden skewer down the middle of each paper to make a billowing sail. Use half a ripe olive and a sliver of carrot to make a flag (*Fig. 2*).

Fig. 1

Fig. 2

TREASURE ISLAND CHIPS AND DIP

Land ho! Yonder lies an island shaded by green pepper palms, inhabited by carrot parrots, and surrounded by cucumber sea turtles. Onshore, pirates can dip into a creamy pool of onions and dill. This edible piece of artwork doubles as a party centerpiece and is guaranteed to fascinate the guests.

Ingredients:
1 large cabbage
GREEN PEPPER PALM TREES (instructions follow)
CARROT PARROTS (instructions follow)
CUCUMBER TURTLES (instructions follow)
TURNIP GARDENIAS (instructions follow)
toothpicks
GREEN ONION DILL DIP (recipe follows)
zucchini, celery, and carrot sticks
potato chips
Makes 12 servings

Directions:
Because decorations need to be soaked in ice water, prepare them overnight and assemble the island the morning of the party.

1. Make a cut across the bottom of the cabbage so that it will sit flat on a platter.

2. Hollow out a well in the center of the cabbage for dip.

3. Shred pieces of cut cabbage like grass to surround the cabbage.

4. Use toothpicks to anchor green pepper palm trees around the sides of the cabbage.

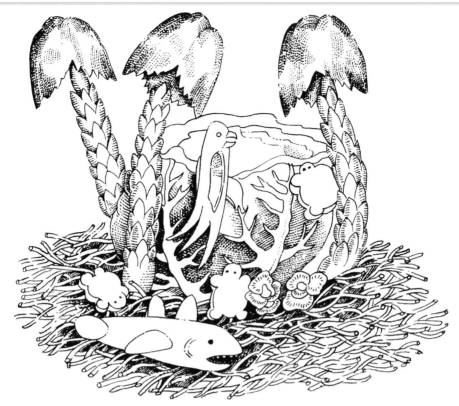

Fig. 1

5. Stick carrot parrots into the cabbage and put turtles around on the grass. You can also use a toothpick to stick a cucumber turtle crawling up the side of the island.

6. Fill the well with dip and surround the platter with zucchini, celery, carrot sticks, and potato chips (*Fig. 1*).

Green Pepper Palm Trees

1. Peel 3 large carrots and cut small gashes in rows up the sides (*Fig. 2*).

2. Cut 3 green peppers so that each "lobe" looks like a palm frond (*Fig. 3*).

3. Soak carrots and green peppers overnight in ice water.

4. Once they've spread open, attach green peppers to the tops of carrots, using toothpicks (*Fig. 4*).

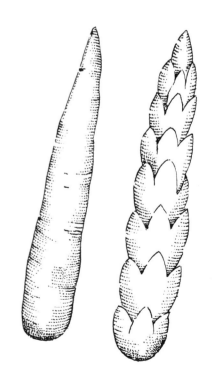

Fig. 2

Fig. 3

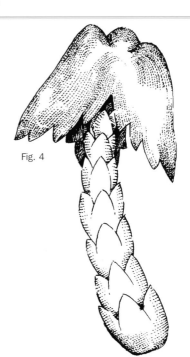

Fig. 4

Carrot Parrots

1. Peel 3 or 4 very small carrots.

2. Cut 3 gashes, about $1^1/2$ inches deep, at the pointed end (*Fig. 5*).

3. Soak in ice water overnight to make "tail feathers" spread.

4. Use pieces of toothpick in sides of carrots for wings.

5. Insert whole cloves for eyes and slivered almonds for bills. Use toothpicks for legs (*Fig. 6*).

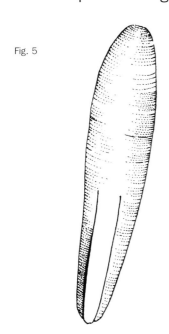

Fig. 5

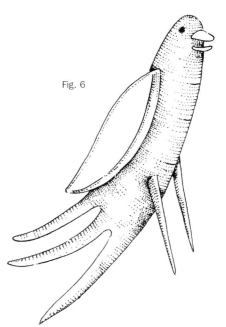

Fig. 6

Cucumber Turtles

1. Slice 2 cucumbers in half lengthwise and cut into quarters.

2. Scoop out seeds and pulp.

3. Carve sections into ovals, then shape into turtles (*Fig. 7*).

4. Score grooves into cucumbers to resemble a shell pattern.

Turnip Gardenias

1. Slice turnips into thin shavings and soak in ice water until they begin to "ruffle."

2. Skewer 4 or 5 slices onto a toothpick.

3. Add a chunk of turnip for the stamen and cover toothpick with a scallion stem (*Fig. 8*).

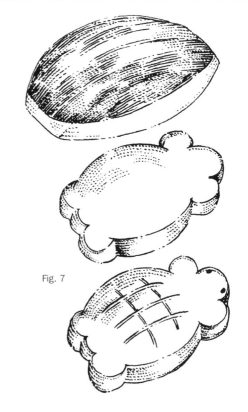

Fig. 7

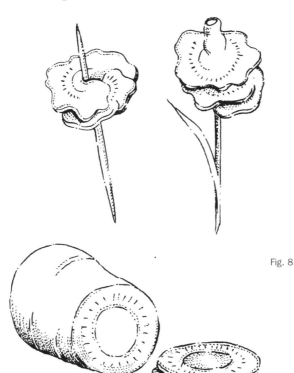

Fig. 8

Cucumber Shark

Fig. 9

1. Cut a gash at one end of a cucumber for a shark mouth.

2. Make cuts behind the mouth for gills.

3. Slice off each side of the tail end and cut a slice from the bottom of the cucumber so that it will rest on a flat surface.

4. Trim the cut pieces in the shape of fins and anchor on top and sides with toothpicks.

5. Use sliced almonds in the mouth for teeth (*Fig. 9*).

Green Onion Dill Dip

Combine 1 cup each sour cream and cottage cheese with chives. Add $1/2$ cup chopped scallions, 1 Tbs. fresh (or 1 tsp. dried) dillweed and 1 tsp. Worcestershire sauce. Cover and chill until serving time.

SKULL AND CROSSBONES BROWNIES

These old-fashioned saucepan brownies become an inspired party dessert when decorated with the classic skull and crossbones. By the way, they're not just for pirate parties—how about Halloween! In a hurry? Just substitute a box of brownie mix and a can of fudge frosting.

Ingredients:

5 1-oz. squares unsweetened chocolate
1 cup unsalted butter or margarine
2 cups sugar
4 eggs
1 tsp. vanilla
$1^1/4$ cups all-purpose flour
$1/4$ tsp. baking powder
$1/2$ tsp. salt
1 cup miniature chocolate chips (reserve some from 12-oz.
  bag for decorating cakes)
CHOCOLATE GLAZE (recipe follows)
$4^1/2$-oz. tube white decorator's icing with round writing tip
Makes 12 servings

Directions:

1. Preheat oven to 350°F (180°C). Line a 9 x 13-inch baking pan with baking parchment.

2. Melt chocolate and butter in a large saucepan over low heat. Blend in sugar.

3. Remove from heat and blend in eggs and vanilla.

4. Stir flour, baking powder, and salt together in a separate bowl. Blend into saucepan mixture.

5. Spread batter in prepared pan. Bake 30 minutes or until brownies pull just slightly away from sides. DO NOT OVERBAKE!

6. Cool completely. Cut into 12 squares about 3 x 3 inches.

7. Spread warm glaze evenly over top and sides of brownies, using a metal spatula.

NOTE: If substituting canned frosting, gently heat it in the top of a double boiler over warm water.

8. Allow brownies to cool on a wire rack until glaze is set.

9. Pipe decorating icing with round writing tip to make two crossed bones and a skull, using miniature chocolate chips for eye sockets.

CHOCOLATE GLAZE

Ingredients:

3 1-oz. squares unsweetened chocolate
$1/2$ cup unsalted butter or margarine
3 cups powdered sugar
1 tsp. vanilla
5 to 9 Tbs. warm milk

Directions:

1. Melt chocolate and butter in a saucepan.

2. Blend in powdered sugar and vanilla.

3. Add enough milk to make a smooth, spreadable glaze.

ICE CREAM VOLCANO

Imagine a dessert with all the fireworks of a Caribbean volcano. This isle of ice cream is like a frosty mountain erupting with hot fudge. Without a doubt, this is the grand finale to a buccaneer bash.

Fig. 1

Ingredients:
1 gallon chocolate, coffee, or chocolate
   chip ice cream
2 cups chocolate cookie (or chocolate
   graham cracker) crumbs
1 16-oz. can or jar fudge sauce
1 eggshell half
1 sugar cube, soaked with lemon
   extract
Makes 12 servings

Directions:

1. Use an ice cream scoop to pile a mound of ice cream scoops onto an 8-inch plate, building it up into a volcano shape (*Fig. 1*).

2. Smooth around sides with a spatula and make a depression in the top. Return to the freezer for at least 3 hours.

3. Cover the sides with chocolate cookie crumbs.

4. Wrap with plastic and return to the freezer for at least 8 hours before serving.

5. Just before serving, pour some warmed fudge sauce in the middle of the depression and allow it to trickle down the sides. Serve the remaining fudge sauce at the table.

6. Set the eggshell half in the depression (hollow side up) and place the sugar cube inside.

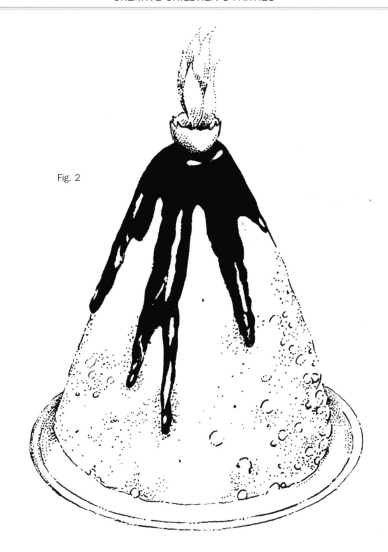

Fig. 2

7. Light the volcano at the table and watch the excitement (*Fig. 2*). When the flame burns down, serve scoops of the volcano with additional warmed fudge sauce (lava) on top. This dessert melts fast, so rush any leftovers back to the freezer for a later encore.

GINGER BREW

Bring soda to the table in a glass pitcher filled with equal parts ginger ale and root beer.

HAPPY CAMPERS PARTY

AGES 7 TO 10

●

Ahhh . . . those lazy, hazy, crazy days of summer camp. The annual ritual has become an American institution for many schoolchildren. Even kids who don't go away to an overnight boarding camp eagerly anticipate the fun activities of a day camp. Now there are camps that specifically cater to children's special interests or talents. When I was a girl, scout camp was my retreat of choice. Some of my fondest and funniest memories come from Camp Timberlake, like the time I was assigned to "tornado watch" (on a beautiful, sunny day) . . . I sat on the roof of our three-sided cabin for hours, waiting to sound an alarm. And who could forget the night my best friend accidentally dropped her transistor radio down the latrine!

MENU

BOX TURTLE
BURGERS

CAMPFIRE ROASTED
POTATOES

TREE TOAD TREATS

FROZEN DIRT BALLS

MOSQUITO SODAS

This HAPPY CAMPERS PARTY makes a great school's-out get-together before friends start going their separate ways for the summer. It works as either a birthday or an "unbirthday" party for "babes of summer." My brother was one of those. His July birthday made it difficult to find school friends still in town, so our family started a tradition of having end-of-school parties. When his real birthday came around, we'd plan a special family day trip as a celebration.

Party Elements

Invitation: Poison Ivy

Decorations: Camp signs, "Please don't feed the bears," backyard tents, firefly tree, bumblebee balloons, "sit-upons"

Party Gear: Camp Silly Swamp Shirts

Instant Involvement: Campfire Sing-along Songs

Games/Activities: White-Water Rafting, Turtle Tug of War, Flowerpot Painting

Goody Bags: Brown Bag Backpacks

 # Invitation: Poison Ivy

Who hasn't come home from camp, or even a nature hike, with a bad case of poison ivy! This paper poison ivy makes a humorous invitation as well as a lesson on what leaves to watch out for.

Materials:

6 9 x 12-inch sheets of green construction paper
pencil
scissors
felt-tip marker
lightweight floral wire
craft glue
floral tape
12 letter-size envelopes
Makes 12 invitations

Directions:

1. Cut 6 3 x 4-inch leaves from each sheet of construction paper. (One sheet of paper will make enough leaves for 2 invitations, with 3 leaves for each.)

2. Write the following messages across one leaf for each invitation:

1st leaf: (your child's name) is just ITCHING for
(guest's name) to attend CAMP SILLY SWAMP
2nd leaf: on (date), at (time) (your address)
3rd leaf: RSVP (your phone number)
BE PREPARED TO GET MUDDY

---

3. Cut wire into a 9-inch length for each leaf.

4. Glue a wire to the back of each leaf, using a small thread of glue (*Fig. 1*).

5. Cover glue with a strip of floral tape and wrap down stem (*Fig. 2*). Allow glue to set.

6. Wrap the stems of each set of three leaves together with floral tape (*Fig. 3*). Leaves may be repositioned by bending wires to fit in envelopes.

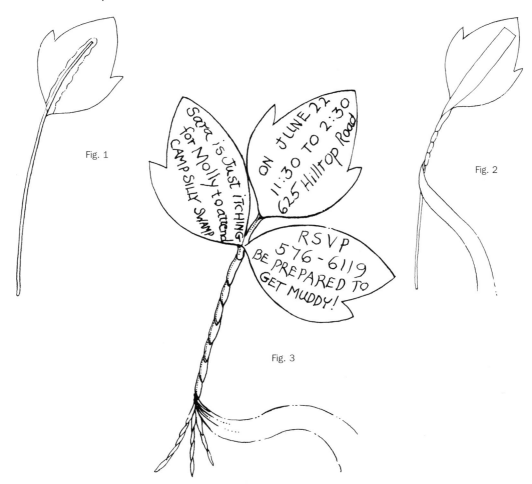

Fig. 1

Fig. 2

Fig. 3

Decorations

This is one party you really want to plan on holding outdoors. (You may even decide to have a rain check date on the invitation.) Post signs along the approach to your house, with a countdown to the campground in blocks, using the Silly Swamp logo on top of each (*Fig. 1*). Greet arriving guests with a banner that goes across the drive announcing: WELCOME TO CAMP SILLY SWAMP (*Fig. 2*). Nail signs to a post or a tree indicating the "NATURE TRAIL" that leads kids around to the backyard. Another sign on the post can give directions to the

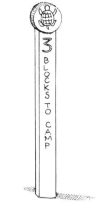

Fig. 1

Fig. 2

LATRINE (*Fig. 3*). Designate a bathroom inside your house and hang a moon on the door. Pitch a camping tent or two to add atmosphere. (You can always borrow one from a friend or neighbor.) Gather a bunch of teddy bears under a tree. Put out a bag full of marshmallows labeled "PLEASE DON'T FEED THE BEARS!" Hang balloons from the trees that have been decorated with the CAMP SILLY SWAMP logo (a turtle, *Fig. 4*), painted in tempera. In place of a party table, the center of activity should

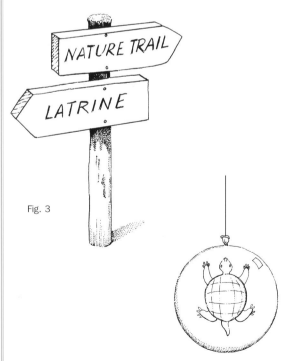

Fig. 3

Fig. 4

be around the "campfire." Set one up surrounded by a circle of stones or bricks. When I was in scouts we sat on mats called "sit-upons" and listened to stories, sang songs, and ate all of our meals from a tin plate. You can personalize the sit-upons with each

Fig. 5

guest's name as well as using little pup tent-shaped place markers (*Fig. 5*). If you can't find metal plates, pie tins work just as well.

Party Gear: Camp Silly Swamp Shirts

This is a project that the whole family can get involved with. You can draw the basic logo and do the writing on the transfer sheets. Let your child fill in the lines with crayon. Once the sheets are made, you simply iron them on the shirts. Just be sure the writing is backwards, because it is reversed on the shirt. However, don't be too hard on yourself if you forget—backwards language just might be right in keeping with CAMP SILLY SWAMP!

Materials:

12 cotton T-shirts (natural or off-white)
12 sheets of iron-on crayon transfer paper
crayons: brown, black, light green, dark green, red, and blue
Makes 12 T-shirts

Directions:

You can use a computer scanner or photocopier to make all of the logos the same, or you can do it freehand. (This can be especially charming because every shirt is similar but unique.)

1. Looking at the pattern, outline the turtle in brown and the CAMP SILLY SWAMP lettering in black.

2. Fill in the legs and the head of the turtle with light green and the shell with dark green.

3. Use a red crayon to fill in the letters of CAMP SILLY SWAMP.

4. Below the logo write the name of the "camper" (*Fig. 1*, page 70).

Fig. 1

5. Before using sheets, be sure to brush off any waxy crayon crumbles; if you don't, you'll end up with unexpected blobs on the shirts. Follow manufacturer's directions for the iron-on transfer procedure.

Instant Involvement: Campfire Sing-along Songs

We all remember singing camp songs. Some seemed to be never-ending, like "The Ants Go Marching" or "99 Bottles of Beer on the Wall." Others were more sentimental, like "Michael, Row Your Boat Ashore," or "500 Miles away from Home." The tradition behind a campfire chorus is that it brings everyone closer together. This makes it an ideal opening activity to a party. As each child arrives, give him or her a plastic plate ukulele. (Simply make 4 sets of notches on opposite sides of a plate and loop rubber bands around the plate for strings.) Kids can sit and strum to the music as part of the sing-along. When guests start to arrive, begin with familiar songs and change some lyrics to fit CAMP SILLY SWAMP (like "The Turtles Go Marching" or "99 Turtles Crawl Up the Wall"). Once those songs have run their course, go around the circle and ask for requests. Meanwhile, make use of the campfire by offering the happy campers skewers of marsh-mallows and pineapple chunks to toast as an "appetizer course."

Games/Activities

FLOWERPOT PAINTING

Paint on clay pots dries amazingly fast because the moisture is rapidly absorbed. By the time the campers are ready to go home, so will their flowerpot projects. Set up a craft area and give each child a small clay flowerpot or several mini-pots to paint. (Be sure to initial all pots on the bottom in advance. Kids get to be very picky about who takes home whose.) Provide kids with acrylic paints, brushes, and sponges and let them express themselves as if they were working in a ceramics studio. By the end of the party, have the pot(s) ready and waiting to go home, filled with soil and a seed packet tucked inside.

WHITE-WATER RAFTING

This is one of those wonderful sprinkler games where kids enjoy getting a little wet. You'll need a back-and-forth-style sprinkler, a skateboard, and something to use as a paddle. (It could be a baseball bat or an old tennis racket—anything that works to "row" the skateboard "raft" along.) Have the players line up single file at one end of the driveway or a paved surface. Turn the sprinkler on so that it moves back and forth. The pressure should be such that (with proper timing) a player could move underneath the overhead stream of water without getting wet. The players take turns sitting on the skateboard and rowing around the sprinkler, trying to stay in sync with the spray so that they're always moving under the crest of the sprinkler spray. Once a player has gone around, he or she goes to the back of the line and gives the raft and paddle to the next child in line. The object of the game is that the driest player at the finish wins. Obviously, the kids may interpret this differently and purposely try to get wet. Of course, that's what spontaneous fun is all about!

TURTLE TUG OF WAR

Another sprinkler game—this time you can play it on the grass. Divide the players into two tribes of turtles. (Remember how camps always gave different age groups of kids tribal names?) The sprinkler should be set at its lowest angle, spraying in one direction. You'll need a long, sturdy rope and a starting signal. Tribes line up on opposite sides of the sprinkler's path and grab their end of the rope. The tug of war begins . . . and ends with the losing team getting dragged through the spray.

NOTE: Both these games can be played dry, if you prefer. Change the rules of White-Water Rafting to use an obstacle course of large plastic soda bottles. Measure each child's speed against a stopwatch, deducting 10 seconds for any bottles that are knocked over. Turtle Tug of War becomes traditional tug of war.

PHOTO OPS

Try to get individual photos of children painting flowerpots or making their way under the sprinkler spray of "White-Water Falls" on a skateboard canoe for thank-you notes. The sing-along and tug of war make great group shots for your photo album.

 ## Goody Bags: Brown Bag Backpacks

Decorate brown lunch bags with the CAMP SILLY SWAMP logo. Fill with granola bars, small sacks of trail mix, and gummy worms. Make up little bags of chocolate-covered raisins and label "CHOCOLATE-COVERED ANTS." You can do the same thing with yellow-green jelly beans, labeling them "LIGHTNING BUGS." Make up a s'mores kit with some graham crackers, marshmallows, and chocolate bars for each bag. Include trinkets like toy harmonicas, compasses, or mini flashlights. Fold flap of bag down and staple ribbon straps in place.

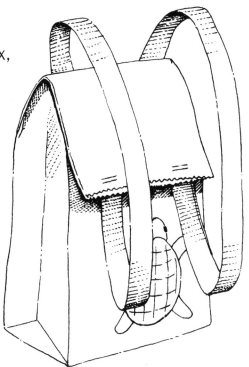

 # Recipes

BOX TURTLE BURGERS

Collecting box turtles is one of those childhood rites of passage. I always brought home a turtle or two among my summer camp souvenirs. All the kids in the neighborhood used to keep their turtles in window wells. Of course, during a big rainstorm we'd have to remember to go out and rescue our pets! Looking back, it might have been more humane if I'd left "Groford" back on the nature trail where I found him. Groford was my inspiration for CAMP SILLY SWAMP's logo and these box turtle burgers. The buns only look difficult to bake. They're actually made from jumbo refrigerator biscuits.

Ingredients:

3 16.3-oz. cans jumbo biscuits (8 to a can)
raisins
2 lbs. ground beef or turkey
condiments: pickles, ketchup, and mustard
Makes 12 servings

Directions:

1. Preheat oven to 375°F (180°C). Have ready 2 to 3 ungreased large baking sheets, since 4 to 6 turtles will take up one sheet. Open only one can of biscuits at a time to work with, since dough gets sticky.

2. FOR EACH TURTLE: Cut one biscuit as shown (*Fig. 1*).

3. Pinch ends of dough marked "head" together to form a head (*Fig. 2*) and tuck firmly under a big biscuit (*Fig. 3*).

4. Tuck legs under biscuit and score across top of biscuit with a very sharp knife.

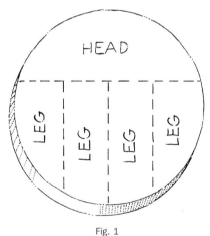

HEAD

LEG LEG LEG LEG

Fig. 1

Fig. 2

Fig. 3

Fig. 4

5. Press raisins in sides of head for eyes (*Fig. 4*).

6. Space turtles at least 2 inches apart on baking sheets. Bake one sheet at a time for 11 to 13 minutes or until golden brown. (TIP: I always "double pan" when baking biscuits so they won't burn on the bottom. This is done by placing an extra baking sheet underneath the one with the dough.)

7. Carefully remove turtles from pan by sliding a thin, flexible metal spatula underneath each one, so as not to break off any legs. Just before serving, slice through top half of biscuit to use as a hamburger bun.

8. Shape ground meat into 12 thin 3-oz. patties. If using the campfire, you can grill these over coals in a grilling basket; indoors, broil or panfry. Be sure burgers are cooked until juices run clear.

9. Serve on turtle buns with condiments.

CAMPFIRE ROASTED POTATOES

Slow-roasted foil-wrapped potatoes were a campfire classic from my childhood. However, it sometimes seemed to take all day for those Idahos to bake over coals. I've since come up with an equally tasty version that's prebaked in the oven. Kids love opening these surprise packages bursting with cheddar cheese and chives.

Ingredients:

12 baking potatoes
1/3 cup softened butter or margarine
3 cups grated cheddar cheese
1/3 cup snipped fresh chives
paprika
Makes 12 servings

Directions:

1. Preheat oven to 375°F (190°C).

2. Wash potatoes and roast directly on oven rack for 45 to 50 minutes.

3. Remove hot potatoes from oven and cut a lengthwise slit in the top of each one, allowing steam to escape. Let cool.

4. Split each potato almost in half and spread open.

5. Blend butter, cheese, and chives together and divide equally among potatoes.

6. Fold potato halves back together and wrap tightly in aluminum foil.

7. Place over hot coals for 15 to 20 minutes or until potatoes are piping hot and cheese is melted.

TREE TOAD TREATS

I can't imagine a more soothing sound than the rhythmic chirping of tree toads on a summer evening. "Peepers," as we called them, were like the sound track to summer camp. I wish I had a recording of them. I'd play it every night to lull myself to sleep.

Ingredients:

12 STIR-AND-BAKE COCOA CUPCAKES (recipe follows) or
     use half of a prepared mix
12 Vienna Fingers sandwich cookies
1 16-oz. can chocolate frosting
1 16-oz. can vanilla frosting
green paste food coloring
2 small pastry bags with coupling nozzles
#2, #4, and #10 round writing tips
Makes 12 servings

**Tree Toad Treats
(recipe pages 76–78)**

Coconut Ice Cream Koalas
(recipe pages 96–97)

Directions:

1. Reserve about $1/4$ cup chocolate frosting for decorating faces of toads. Use the rest to frost tops of cupcakes.

2. Tint vanilla frosting green.

3. Cut Vienna Fingers in half crosswise and sandwich together with some green frosting (*Fig. 1*).

4. Place one on top of each cupcake and frost with green frosting, completely coating cookies.

5. Fill one of the pastry bags with the remaining green frosting.

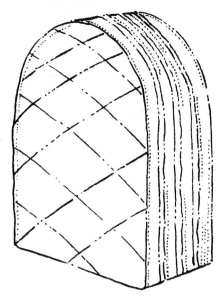

Fig. 1

Fig. 2

Fig. 3

6. Attach the #10 writing tip and pipe looplike hind legs at sides of cookies and 2 ball shapes at top of cookies for eyes (*Fig. 2*).

7. Remove the #10 writing tip and attach the #4 writing tip. Pipe front legs on toads and add toes to back and front legs.

8. Fill the remaining pastry bag with reserved chocolate frosting. Attach a #2 writing tip and pipe pupils on eyes and mouth (*Fig. 3*).

STIR-AND-BAKE COCOA CUPCAKES

Ingredients:
$1^2/3$ cups all-purpose flour
1 cup sugar
$1/4$ cup Dutch-process cocoa
1 tsp. baking soda
$1/2$ tsp. salt
1 cup water
$1/3$ cup vegetable oil
1 tsp. vinegar
1 tsp. salt
Makes 12 cupcakes

Directions:
1. Preheat oven to 325°F (160°C). Line 12 cupcake cups with liners.

2. Combine flour, sugar, cocoa, baking soda, and salt in a mixing bowl.

3. Combine water, oil, vinegar, and vanilla in a glass measuring cup and beat with a fork.

4. Stir liquid into dry ingredients, using fork to beat until completely blended.

5. Fill each cupcake liner two-thirds full.

6. Bake cupcakes 25 to 30 minutes or until a toothpick inserted in the center comes out clean. Cool completely.

FROZEN DIRT BALLS

Mud pies, clay cakes . . . call them whatever you like. Whether in a swamp or a sandbox, kids love to make awful-looking culinary creations out of inedible ingredients. The only difference between these dirt balls and the summer-camp kind is that they're yummy instead of yukky. In fact, they're so much fun that you might want to let the kids make their own.

Ingredients:

1 gallon chocolate or coffee ice cream
3 to 4 cups finely crushed chocolate wafers, Oreo cookies,
   or chocolate graham crackers
gummy worms
raisins
large ice cream scoop (#100 food scoop)
Makes 12 servings

Directions:

1. Cover a tray with aluminum foil.

2. Make 12 large scoops of ice cream and place on foil.

3. Return to freezer for at least 30 minutes so ice cream will be easier to work with. (This is especially important if you're bringing the dessert outside for the kids to make their own.)

4. Place cookie crumbs in a shallow pan and roll ice cream balls in crumbs, coating thoroughly.

5. Stick gummy worms and raisins (ants) in dirt balls. Serve immediately or return to freezer.

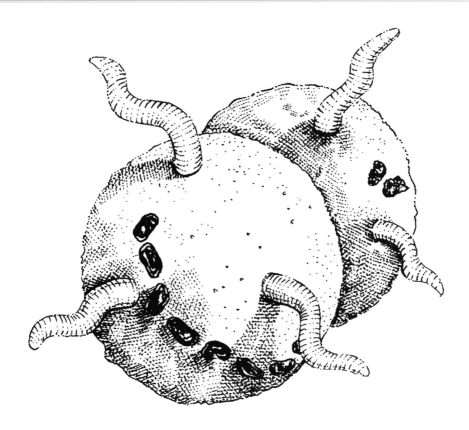

MOSQUITO SODAS

Relabel cans of assorted flavors of soda pop as the "Mosquito" brand. Use color-coordinated construction paper, such as purple for grape, green for lemon-lime, brown for cola, and orange for orange. Cut paper to fit around cans and write:

**Mmm . . .
MOSQUITO
the soda with
a Buzzz**

---

on each paper. Tape around cans. You can also label large, economy-size bottles in the same way. Serve sodas over ice or chill cans in the refrigerator, since you obviously can't throw paper-labeled cans into an ice chest.

BOOMERANG BARBECUE

AGES 7 TO 11

●

G'day, mates! Here's a big "shivoo" (Australian for celebration). All the adventure of the wondrous world down under, with its incredible collection of wacky wildlife and cuddly creatures, come together in this Boomerang Barbecue. From wallabies to wombats, lorries to lyrebirds, dingoes to dugongs . . . the animals of Australia are one of the greatest marvels on earth.

For this party, guests receive a boomerang invitation, beckoning them to an outback barbecue for dining on such delicacies as Tasmanian devil dogs, kangaroo "karrot kake," and ice cream koalas. They don Aussie bush hats, paint Aboriginal-style art, and play goofy games like a kangaroo race, a kiwi roll, and a sheepherding contest. A Boomerang Bash can be appreciated by that upper age range that often feels a little too "grown-up" for theme parties . . . and why not? It's even a great theme for grown-up parties.

MENU

TASMANIAN DEVIL DOGS ON BOOMERANG BUNS

SYDNEY-STYLE SPUDS

KANGAROO "KARROT KAKE"

COCONUT ICE CREAM KOALAS

BRISBANE KIWI BREEZE

Party Elements

Invitation: Boomerang Cards

Decorations: Australian bush signs, travel posters, Australian animal character cutouts, map of the continent tablecloth, Great Barrier Reef coral collection, Aboriginal "pottery" place settings

Party Gear: Aussie-style Bush Hats

Instant Involvement: Primitive Bark Painting

Games/Activities: Kangaroo Race, Kiwi Roll, Sheepherding

Goody Bags: Outback Survival Bags

Invitation: Boomerang Cards

Materials:

12 sheets of light brown construction
    paper
pencil, black crayon or marker that
    won't bleed through paper
scissors
oversized envelopes
    (at least 9 inches
    x 7 inches)
Makes 12 cards

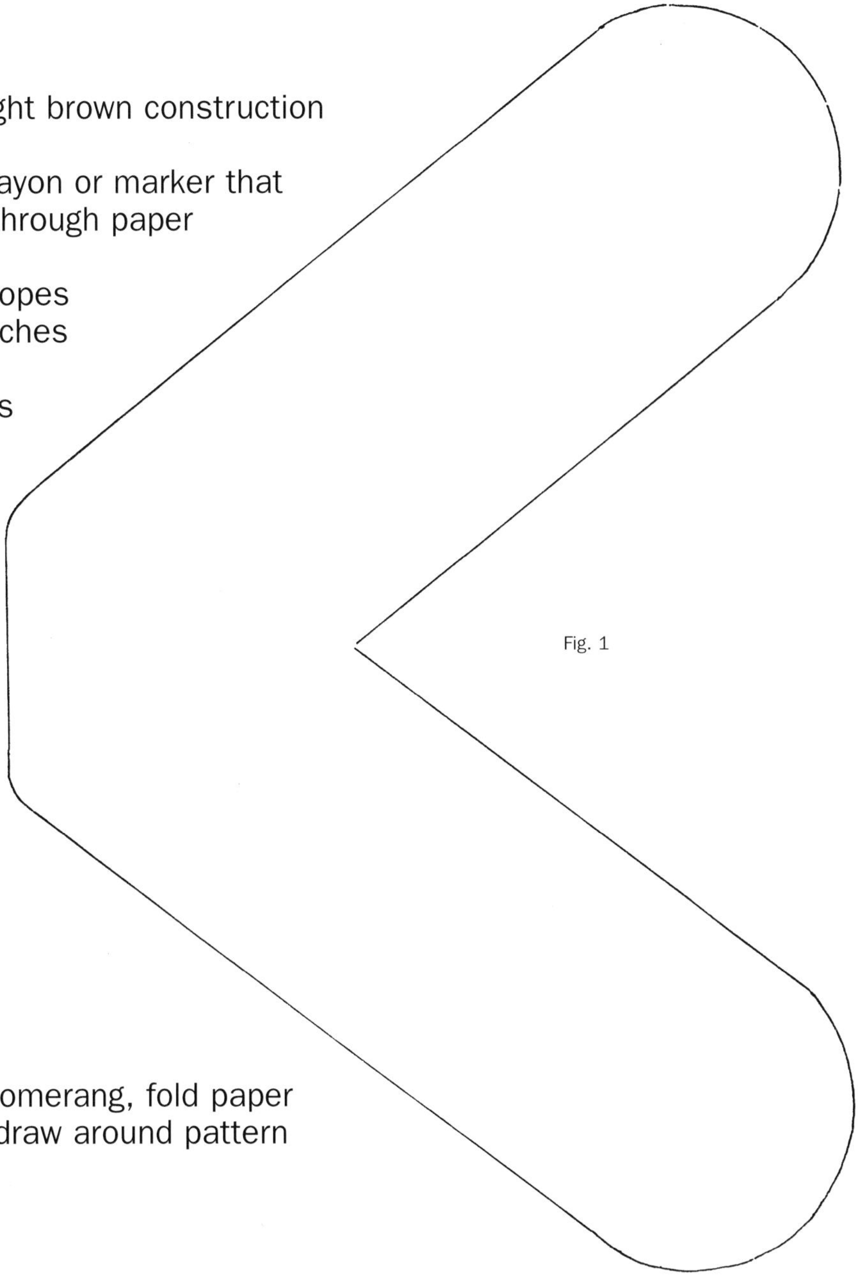

Fig. 1

Directions:

1. For each boomerang, fold paper
in half and draw around pattern
(*Fig. 1*).

2. Be sure that the center of the boomerang is backed up against the fold so the invitation will open and shut (*Fig. 2*).

3. Cut out along dotted line (*Fig. 3*).

4. Across the front of each invitation, write:

A BOOMERANG ALWAYS RETURNS TO WHERE IT CAME FROM
PLEASE COME BACK WITH (invited guest's name)
TO A BOOMERANG BARBECUE IN THE OUTBACK

Inside, write:

FOR AN AUSTRALIAN BARBECUE IN HONOR OF (your child's name)
ON (date and time), **AT** (your address)
RSVP (your phone number)

---

5. Mail boomerangs in envelopes (*Fig. 4*).

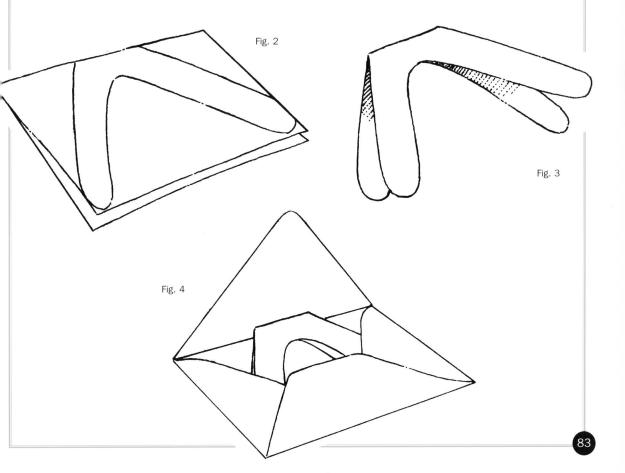

Fig. 2

Fig. 3

Fig. 4

Decorations

Australia is both an island continent and a country with diverse terrain and climate. The lush vegetation of the eastern coast is in stark contrast to the desert interior. There are sunny, sandy beaches near Sydney and snow-covered alps near Canberra. Geographical wonders range from the colorful coral of the Great Barrier Reef to the massive Ayers Rock, which rises from the stark desert of the northern territory.

The "Outback" pretty much describes most of Australia, since anywhere beyond the populous coastal regions is very rugged. One of the ways to get your guests into the party spirit is to post some signs along the road leading up to your house, such as: "ENTERING THE BUSH COUNTRY" or "OUTBACK AHEAD—DRIVE AT YOUR OWN RISK" (*Fig. 1*). When they get to your drive you can post a "KANGAROO CROSSING" sign (*Fig. 2*).

Fig. 1

Fig. 2

Fig. 3

Fig. 4

Fig. 5

Fig. 6

Fig. 7

Fig. 8

Fig. 9

Fig. 10

Fig. 11

Create large cardboard cutouts of cartoon-like Australian creatures, giving the characters names: "Captain Wallaby" (*Fig. 3*), "Willy Wombat" (*Fig. 4*), "Dingo Dog" (*Fig. 5*), "Plato Platypus" (*Fig. 6*), "Amy Emu" (*Fig. 7*), "Piwi Kiwi" (*Fig. 8*), "Lyle Lyrebird" (*Fig. 9*), "Coco Cockatoo" (*Fig. 10*), and "King Koala" (*Fig. 11*).

Fig. 12

Drape the party table with a large map of Australia, drawn with a brown marker on a cream or beige paper or plastic tablecloth (brown on beige looks like an old map). Provide sets of crayons or markers for each child to color in areas of the map where they are seated. Stuffed animal or plastic toy kangaroos or koala bears can be worked into a centerpiece, along with branches of eucalyptus leaves (a koala bear's favorite food). Have any coral around the house from a vacation shell collection? If so, use it to decorate the party table. Some of the most beautiful coral in the world comes from the Great Barrier Reef.

Sheep ranching is synonymous with Australia, so make a whole herd of woolly place cards: Cut 9 x 12-inch construction paper into $4^1/2$ x 6-inch rectangles. Fold tent-style and draw face and legs of sheep with crayons or marker. Glue on cotton balls to make the rest of the body and head. Write each child's name on a card (*Fig. 12*). Decorate plates and cups with Aborigine-style art, using nontoxic crayons or markers. These primitive-looking paintings depicting wildlife, hunters, fish, turtles, and other figures are copied by Australian artisans as popular pottery designs (*Fig. 13*).

Fig. 13

Party Gear: Aussie-style Bush Hats

Many types of hats lend themselves to creating the "Crocodile Dundee" look. For example, you can stick a tuft of feathers in the band of a Panama hat. However, I prefer the pinned-up brim style you can model from a simple cowboy hat. As long as the hat is made from *flexible* fabric or straw, it will work just fine. Many party suppliers carry such hats, and they're often cheaper by the dozen. For feathers, choose natural bird feathers such as pheasant, duck, or turkey as opposed to dyed chicken feathers. These often come in bulk bags. You'll need 2 to 3 dozen feathers (2 or 3 feathers per hat).

Materials:

12 inexpensive felt or straw cowboy
   hats with flexible brims
craft feathers (in natural bird colors)
pins
craft glue, aluminum foil
buttonhole silk twist thread, large
   needle or embroidery needle
12 leather or wood-look buttons with 2 or 4
   holes (do not use shank-style buttons)
Makes 12 hats

Fig. 1

Directions:

1. If there's a depression in the crown of the hats, press it out with your hand.

2. Pin up one side of each hat (*Fig. 1*). Make a "fan" of 2 or 3 feathers, securing the ends of quills with a drop of glue (*Fig. 2*). Allow feather fans to dry on foil.

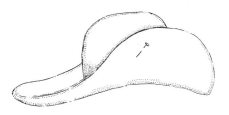

Fig. 2

3. When dry, glue quill tips of feathers to the side of the folded brim.

4. Sewing through all layers of the hat, sew button over quills so that they are anchored in place by the button, and the button anchors the brim against the crown (*Fig. 3*).

Fig. 3

Instant Involvement: Primitive Bark Painting

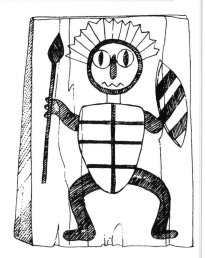

The Aborigines were the original Australians. Anthropologists believe that they arrived on the continent over 12,000 years ago from the islands of Southeast Asia. Many of the tribes were nomads and moved from place to place, following their sources of food and water (like many of our Native American tribes). Their artwork was both primitive and beautiful in its simplicity. It usually depicted the wildlife they relied on: emus, kangaroos, fish, turtles—or the hunters themselves. Today many Australian artisans copy the Aboriginal style as decorative designs on pottery and crafts.

The Aborigines were known for bark painting. They used slabs of tree bark and frayed twigs or sticks for paintbrushes. This makes a great get-acquainted project for arriving guests. Set up a "Primitive Bark Painting Workshop" to involve incoming

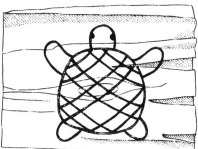

guests. Of course, unless you have a forest in your back-yard, stripping bark from trees isn't all that practical. Cedar shakes (shingles) make perfect natural canvases. They're readily available from home improvement stores or lumber-yards. You can use regular paintbrushes or, for authenticity, fray the ends of sticks with a knife and use those for brushes. Provide basic colors of acrylic paint along with sample shingles of Aboriginal designs (see examples) to get them started.

Games/Activities

Fig. 1

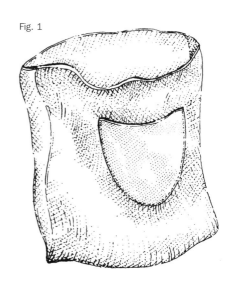

KANGAROO RACE

This is a wacky sack race where players pretend that they're kangaroos. For kangaroo sacks, you'll first need two sturdy burlap potato sacks. (I know, it can be hard finding such old-fashioned items in this day and age. In a pinch, I've sewn my own out of burlap from the craft store. If you go that route, be sure to reinforce the seams with several rows of stitches.) The top of each potato sack should be open. Sew a felt patch on the front for a kangaroo pouch (*Fig. 1*). For the joey, you can use beanbag baby kangaroos or make your own out of a stuffed sock with felt ears and a shoe button nose and eyes (*Fig. 2*). To start the relay, divide players into two teams and have them line up single file, with teams side by side. At the opposite end of the yard or room, "plant a eucalyptus tree" (that is, put eucalyptus branches in a pot or vase). Give the first player in line on each team a kangaroo sack with a joey in the pouch. At the starting signal, players get into their sacks and begin hopping towards, around, and back from the eucalyptus tree. If the joey falls out of a player's pouch, that player has to pick it up, put it back in his pouch, return to the starting position, and start all over again. When a player completes a lap around the tree and returns to the team, he jumps out of the sack and turns it over to the next player in line. The first team to finish wins.

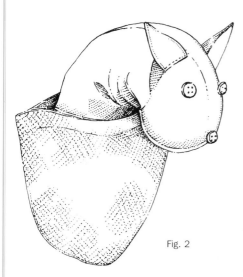

Fig. 2

KIWI ROLL

This race is an Australian version of the classic "egg roll" played on Easter. Instead of using colorful dyed eggs, substitute fuzzy brown kiwifruit (kiwis are also much more durable than Easter eggs).

Establish a start and finish line. Line players up side by side across the starting line. At the starting signal, players get on their hands and knees and use their nose to roll the kiwi to the finish line. (If you are playing indoors or have just a short distance to go, make the race last longer by using the finish line as a turnaround point and finishing back at the starting line.) Obviously, the first player to finish the race wins the kiwi roll.

NOTE: A cute prize for this is a small plastic loving cup with a kiwi stuck inside.

SHEEPHERDING

Australia is known for its sheep ranches and is a major world supplier of wool. In this game, players "herd their sheep" from the starting line to the finish line. For sheep, each player has a flock of a dozen cotton balls. You'll need to play indoors on a smooth floor, or use a paved driveway. At the starting signal, kids get down on their hands and knees and blow their sheep across the floor (or driveway) with a straw. The first player to herd all of his or her sheep over the finish line is the winner.

PHOTO OPS

Take individual pictures of kids in their Aussie-style bush hats, displaying their original Aboriginal bark paintings. These make great photos to enclose with thank-you notes. Ground-level shots of goofy races like the kiwi roll and sheepherding also make entertaining photos.

Goody Bags: Outback Survival Bags

Decorate different-colored sacks with Aboriginal-style art designs (see *Decorations* or *Primitive Bark Painting*). On the front write "OUTBACK SURVIVAL BAG." Fill bags with granola bars, compass, kiwi-flavored hard candies or jelly beans, dried papaya spears, and gummy snakes or worms. Photocopy maps of Australia and fold up with a small pack of crayons or markers so the kids can color them. Include a bean-bag toy kangaroo or a toy jeep. Fold down the tops of bags and punch a series of three holes across the top. Thread a twig through the holes as a closure.

 # Recipes

TASMANIAN DEVIL DOGS ON BOOMERANG BUNS

These kid-pleasing kabobs are really just baby franks on a skewer, served up Australian style on boomerang-shaped buns with Tasmanian Devil Sauce. You can either use cocktail franks or simply cut your favorite brand of regular franks into quarters.

Ingredients:

2 16-oz. packages of cocktail franks (or substitute 2 16-oz. packages of regular-size franks, cut in quarters)
2 red bell peppers, cut into 1-inch pieces
2 green bell peppers, cut into 1-inch pieces
2 yellow bell peppers, cut into 1-inch pieces
2 16-oz. jars chunk-style bread and butter pickles (or cut spears into chunks)
TASMANIAN DEVIL SAUCE (recipe follows)
BOOMERANG BUNS (recipe follows)
Makes 12 servings

Directions:

1. For each kabob, thread cocktail franks, bell peppers, and pickle chunks alternately on skewers (if using wooden skewers, cover exposed ends with pieces of foil so they won't burn).

2. Baste kabobs lightly with sauce.

3. Grill over coals or broil until lightly charred and franks are heated through.

4. Serve with sliced boomerang buns and additional sauce on the side.

TASMANIAN DEVIL SAUCE

Ingredients:

2 12-oz. bottles of chili sauce
2 Tbs. soy sauce
2 Tbs. cider vinegar
1 6-oz. can frozen pineapple juice concentrate, thawed
2 Tbs. brown sugar
1 tsp. dry mustard

Directions:

1. Combine all ingredients in a saucepan and bring to boil.

2. Simmer 3 to 5 minutes, or until slightly thickened.

BOOMERANG BUNS

Ingredients:

2 10-oz. cans soft breadsticks
1 egg beaten with 1 Tbs. water

Directions:

1. Preheat oven to 350°F (180°C). Cover 2 large baking sheets with baking parchment.

2. Open cans of breadsticks and separate into strips.

3. Arrange 3 inches apart on baking sheets, bending at an angle so that they resemble boomerangs.

4. Brush with egg mixture and bake 12 to 14 minutes or until golden brown.

5. Split buns open lengthwise (like "bent" hot dog buns).

SYDNEY-STYLE SPUDS

Fed up with fries? Why not throw a few yams on the barbie . . . that's what Crocodile Dundee does. (Of course, he serves grilled snakes along with his spuds.) These make a great side dish for an outback barbecue—that is, the potatoes, not the snakes!

Ingredients:

8–10 medium-size sweet potatoes or yams
1 fresh pineapple, cut into 1-inch chunks (you may substitute canned pineapple)
SYDNEY SAUCE (recipe follows)
sesame seeds
Makes 12 servings

Directions:

1. Preheat oven to 375°F (190°C). Wash potatoes and pierce with fork to allow the steam to escape.

2. Place potatoes directly on oven rack and bake 40 minutes. Cool completely.

3. Cut potatoes into chunks, leaving skin on.

4. Thread on skewers alternately with pineapple chunks.

5. Brush with SYDNEY SAUCE and sprinkle with sesame seeds. Grill over hot coals or broil until glazed and sesame seeds are golden brown. (Watch carefully—do not burn!)

SYDNEY SAUCE

Ingredients:

2 Tbs. melted butter
3 Tbs. sesame oil
2 Tbs. lime juice
1 tsp. soy sauce

$^1/_4$ tsp. ground ginger
$^1/_4$ tsp. cinnamon
$^1/_3$ cup honey

Directions:

Combine all ingredients in a small bowl or measuring cup.

KANGAROO "KARROT KAKE"

Watch the kids bounce up and down when you carry this cake out of the kitchen. Since kangaroos are a beige-brown, I've used a cinnamon-mocha-flavored frosting. However, the peanut butter frosting on page 28 is also a good kangaroo color.

Ingredients:

$^1/_2$ cup boiling water
2 Tbs. instant coffee
2 cups grated carrot
2 cups all-purpose flour
$1^1/_4$ cups firmly packed dark brown sugar
$1^1/_4$ tsp. baking soda
1 tsp. salt
1 tsp. cinnamon
1 tsp. nutmeg
1 tsp. vanilla
$^1/_2$ cup vegetable oil
3 eggs
SPICY MOCHA FROSTING (recipe follows)
$4^1/_2$-oz. tube chocolate decorator frosting with round writing tip
2 whole unblanched almonds
Makes 12 generous servings

Directions:

1. Blend coffee with boiling water.

2. Put carrots in a bowl and pour coffee over carrots. Let stand 10 minutes.

3. Preheat oven to 350°F (180°C). Line a 9 x 13-inch pan with baking parchment.

4. Combine flour, brown sugar, soda, salt, cinnamon, and nutmeg in a large mixing bowl.

5. Add oil, eggs, and carrot mixture.

6. Beat on medium speed 1 minute, scraping bowl frequently, until blended. Beat 2 minutes longer.

7. Pour into pan and bake 45 to 50 minutes. Cool completely.

8. Remove cake from pan by inverting onto a baking sheet and peeling away paper.

9. Cover a 14 x 18-inch board with foil. Cut cake as shown in diagram (*Fig. 1*).

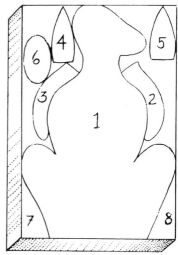

Fig. 1

10. Trim down the thickness of the arms and shape the baby kangaroo head or "joey."

11. Arrange pieces as shown, using some frosting to anchor arms and the head of the joey on top of cake (*Fig. 2*).

12. Cover cake evenly with frosting, smoothing with a metal spatula.

13. Use tube of chocolate decorator's icing to draw the eye, nose, and mouth on the head of the kangaroo and on the joey.

14. Use almonds for the joey's ears (*Fig. 3*).

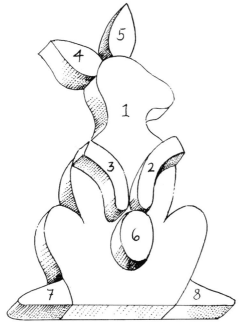

Fig. 2

Fig. 3

SPICY MOCHA FROSTING

Ingredients:

2 Tbs. instant coffee
2 tsp. cinnamon
3 Tbs. water
$5^1/_3$ cups powdered sugar
$2/_3$ cup butter or margarine, softened

Directions:

1. Blend instant coffee and cinnamon with water until dissolved.

2. Combine in a large mixing bowl with powdered sugar and butter. Beat until frosting is a smooth, spreadable consistency.

3. If needed, blend in an extra spoonful or two of water.

COCONUT ICE CREAM KOALAS

This adorable dessert only looks difficult to make. The koalas are simple to assemble and almost too cute to eat!

Ingredients:

1 gallon chocolate or vanilla ice cream
1 14-oz. bag shredded coconut, toasted*
1 16-oz. can chocolate fudge frosting
24 dried banana chips
12 large pecan halves
24 raisins
Pastry bag with coupling nozzle and a #2 or #4 round writing tip
Makes 12 servings

Directions:

1. Cover 2 baking sheets with aluminum foil.

2. Scoop 12 large scoops of ice cream onto one sheet. Return to freezer while preparing ears.

To toast coconut: Preheat oven to 350°F (180°C). Spread coconut on a baking sheet and bake 6 to 8 minutes, stirring 3 times while baking. Watch carefully; coconut burns quickly!

3. Spread each side of one banana chip with a thin layer of fudge frosting.

4. Press coconut into frosting so that ears look "furry" (*Fig. 1*). Place ears in freezer until frosting is firm.

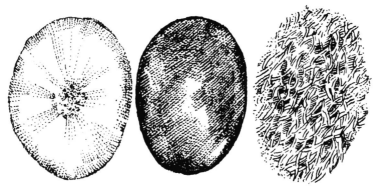

Fig. 1

5. Remove ice cream scoops from freezer and roll in remaining coconut.

6. Insert banana chips into each scoop for ears, uncoated side facing forward.

7. Press raisins into each scoop for eyes and a pecan half for nose.

8. Fill pastry bag with remaining frosting and use to pipe a mouth and nostrils on the pecan half (*Fig. 2*). Return to freezer for at least 2 hours before serving.

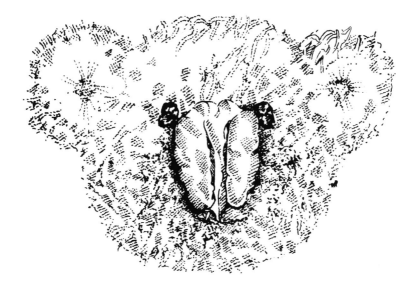

Fig. 2

BRISBANE KIWI BREEZE

Ingredients:

$1/2$ gallon limeade (may be prepared from concentrate)
$1/2$ gallon pineapple juice (may be prepared from concentrate)
$1/2$ gallon lime or kiwi sorbet or sherbet
3 whole kiwis, sliced
12 "silly shaped" straws
Makes 12 generous servings

Directions:

1. Combine limeade and pineapple juice in 1-gallon container and chill until serving time.

2. Pour into tall cups or glasses and top with lime or kiwi sorbet.

3. Cut halfway through to the center of each kiwi slice and hang on the edge of each cup.

ALIEN INVASION PARTY

AGES 8 TO 10

I n 1947 the Air Force allegedly recovered the wreckage of a "flying disc" near Roswell, New Mexico . . . and the world has never been quite the same! Since then, images of alien beings have strangely resembled crash test dummies with large egg-shaped heads and small bodies. It's said that a UFO sighting is reported somewhere on this planet every three minutes. Witnesses are not necessarily wacky; among them are respected historical figures like Alexander Hamilton and Winston Churchill. One popular theory is that the aliens have been observing us for thousands of years and that the similarities between Egyptian and Aztec pyramids are no mere coincidence.

For those with vivid imaginations, an "alien invasion" could mean just about anything—from the hostile takeover in H. G. Wells' *War of the Worlds* to the peaceful-hands-across-the-universe theme of *ET*. Most extraterrestrial enthusiasts believe that there's a massive cover-up on alien activities, making them more than just modern-day mythology. Next to Halloween, an alien invasion is the ultimate costume party. Kids use their creativity to come up with their own versions of what an alien looks like, acts like, and sounds like. After all, the guests will be arriving from different planets in far-off galaxies.

MENU

UFO BAGEL BAR

POD PEOPLE'S CHIPS AND RED PLANET DIP

EXTRATERRESTRIAL AFTER-DINNER MINT CAKE

FROZEN FLYING SAUCERS

ROCKET FUEL

Party Elements

Invitation: X-File

Decorations: FBI warning signs, UFO wreckage, alien crop circles, alien dummies, alien balloons, intergalactic conference room

Party Gear: Planetary Pendants

Instant Involvement: Starship Shop

Games/Activities: Alien Egg Abduction, Asteroid Attack, Time Machine

Goody Bags: Alien Convention Totes

 # Invitation: X-File

Everyone loves to speculate that the government is somehow sequestering top-secret information on alien activities. Supposedly there's a famous file on UFO sightings, extraterrestrials, and unexplainable events. Of course, one of these events will be taking place right under your own roof!

Materials:

12 file folders with tabs
detailed map of your neighborhood
markers or crayons
photo of your child with face made
   up like an alien
12 envelopes, large enough for file
   folders (usually 10 x 13 inches)
Makes 12 invitations

Directions:

On the tab of each file folder write "Alien Invasion." Across the front of each folder write in bold letters **X-FILE.** Also make a notation on the folder that says **"Top Secret FYI"** (*Fig. 1*).

Fig. 1

Inside the folder your child can draw doodles of aliens and UFOs (*Fig. 2*). On an 8^1/$_2$ x 11-inch sheet of paper, write the following message by hand or on a computer:

Fig. 2

THIS REPORT INDICATES ALIEN ACTIVITY IN THE AREA OF (your address). SEVERAL UFOs HAVE BEEN SIGHTED IN THIS REGION, AND WE HAVE JUST RECEIVED CONFIRMATION THAT EXTRATERRESTRIAL BEINGS ARE INHABITING THIS RESIDENCE. PLEASE BE ON THE ALERT FOR THE ALIEN IN THIS PHOTO. HE (she) **USES THE ALIAS** (your child's name) **ON EARTH. DURING THE DAY HE** (she) **ATTENDS** (your child's school) **AND IS OFTEN SEEN IN THE COMPANY OF** (leave this blank to write in the invited guest's name). **WE BELIEVE THAT THESE ALIENS ARE PLANNING A RENDEZVOUS ON** (date and time of party). **THIS NUMBER AND CODE** (your phone number + RSVP) **HAS BEEN INTERCEPTED THROUGH OUR SURVEILLANCE DEVICES.**

Your child's photo can be either photocopied or scanned onto this page. On another page, photocopy or scan the street map and mark a big **X** on the location of your house. You'll need to make 12 copies of each page (or as many as you have invited guests). Put both pages in each file. Mail files in envelopes.

NOTE: When guests RSVP, tell them that they can either come dressed as aliens or in their familiar "human disguise."

Decorations

Fig. 1

For this party, you'll want your house to stand out from the surrounding neighbors' as a residence for an alien rendezvous. Start by putting some signs in the front yard like: "WELCOME TO ROSWELL," "FBI WARNING: THIS AREA OFF LIMITS" or "NO TRESPASSING—PROCEED AT YOUR OWN RISK" (*Fig. 1*). Create some UFO wreckage by making a circle of Christmas lights on the ground. Within the circle, scatter debris like old furnace ducts, scrap metal, pipes, parts from nonfunctioning appliances or

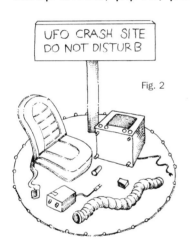

Fig. 2

junked electronic devices. (For example, I still have a defunct 20-year-old black-and-white TV set sitting in the garage.) If you have any children's car seats, put them in the circle; after all, aliens are pretty small. Post a sign that says "UFO CRASH SITE: DO NOT DISTURB" (*Fig. 2*). You can even make some aliens to add to the scene: Stuff body stockings and add heads made from empty gallon bottles of bleach or detergent (*Fig. 3*). These can be propped up at the front door to welcome guests.

The party room should have a sci-fi, hi-tech intergalactic conference table for this important meeting of alien ambassadors. Start by covering the party table with aluminum foil. Tape blinking colored Christmas lights around the edge of the table. Dim the lights and string delicate white Christmas lights on the ceiling or walls to resemble stars and constellations. Styrofoam balls can be painted to resemble planets and hung from the ceiling along with Frisbees or aluminum pie plates for flying

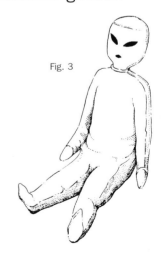

Fig. 3

saucers. Comets can be made by using wads of aluminum foil, trailed by streamers of tinsel; suspend from the ceiling with threads (*Fig. 4*). Place a big world globe (or inflatable "beach ball" globe) in the center of the table. Put an X of tape across the United States along with a little sign that says YOU

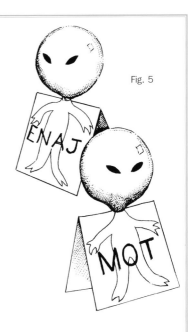

Fig. 5

ARE HERE! (You could also hang a map of the world or the United States on the wall.) Make alien balloon figures for place markers: Cut double-

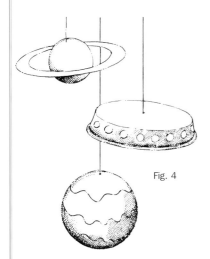

Fig. 4

sided poster board bodies and fold in half with a slit at the neck to insert the balloon head. Draw a face on the balloon and write a name across the body. To make it look like an alien language, write the name backwards (*Fig. 5*).

Party Gear: Planetary Pendants

Give guests ID badges or "Planetary Pendants" to wear around their necks, identifying their names and planets of origin. You can use planets in this solar system or use made-up names of planets from distant solar systems. (If you have 12 guests you're going to have to come up with additional planets anyway.) For extra fun, write the kids' names backwards to resemble an alien language.

Materials:
12 small plastic or sturdy paper cocktail or dessert plates
    (gold, silver, black, or bright colors)
glitter paint in a writing tube (color should contrast with plates)
2 yards of $^3/_4$-inch- to 1-inch-wide striped ribbon
craft glue
Makes 12 pendants

Directions:

1. Use glitter paint to write the guest's name (backwards) and the name of his or her planet. For example, Jane from Jupiter would be: Enaj of Jupiter (*Fig. 1*). You can also make up names for other planets. For example, Tom from the planet Zenox would be Mot of Zenox (*Fig. 2*).

2. Cut ribbon into 1-yard lengths, make a loop for each plate, and glue ends to backs of plates (*Fig. 3*).

3. Allow glue to dry completely. It helps to use a very "tacky" brand. (Finished plate [*Fig. 4*] is for Kevin of Alphor, or Nivek of Alphor.)

Fig. 1

Fig. 2

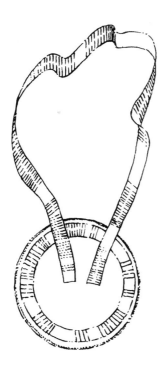

Fig. 3

Fig. 4

Instant Involvement: Starship Shop

You provide the basic structure for flying saucers, and the party guests get to decorate them as soon as they arrive. By the time they're ready to leave, the paint should be dry.

Materials for basic starships:

24 sturdy paper plates
12 sturdy paper bowls
4 egg cartons
craft glue
scissors
Makes 12 starships

Instructions:

1. For each starship, invert a paper plate over the top of a second paper plate, joining around the edges with glue (*Fig. 1*).

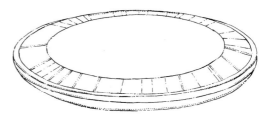

Fig. 1

2. Apply glue around the edge of the bowl and invert over the center of the top plate (*Fig. 2*).

3. Cut egg carton sections apart and glue 4 to the base of each starship for landing gear, applying glue to the edges of the cups (*Fig. 3*).

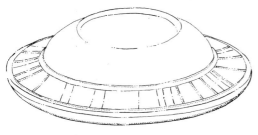

Fig. 2

4. Allow plates to dry thoroughly.

5. Before guests arrive, set up a work area with a starship at each place setting.

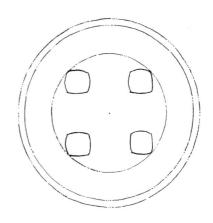

Fig. 3

6. Provide the following materials for the kids to decorate their own:
> tempera or acrylic paints and brushes
> colored glue, craft glue, and glitter
> sequins
> pieces of aluminum and colored foil
> scissors
> pipe cleaners

Demonstrate how to get started. For example, use glitter and sequins for lights, or squares of foil for windows. Pipe-cleaner coils make great radar devices. The aliens will take over from there, becoming engineers of their own original designs (*Fig. 4*).

Fig. 4

 Games/Activities

ALIEN EGG ABDUCTION

This game presumes that all aliens hatch from eggs. The only difference from one planet to the next is in the color of their eggs. This game works well if you divide players into 3 or 4 teams from 3 or 4 planets. Each planet has its own unique color of eggs: Venus (green), Mars (red), Neptune (blue), Pluto (purple). You don't need Easter egg dye kits if they're not in season. Just add a teaspoon of white vinegar and several drops of food coloring to individual cups of boiling water.

Dye about a dozen hard-cooked eggs for each planet. You can then use felt-tip markers to draw spidery veins on the eggs. Hide the eggs randomly around the yard. Divide the players into planetary teams. Explain to them that an evil alien airship abducted eggs from their planets and hid them on Earth. Give each team color-coded "specimen" bags and send them out to hunt just for their eggs. The first planetary team to recover all of their eggs wins—but it's just as much fun to let the game continue until all of the eggs have been found.

ASTEROID ATTACK

In this game, players are told that a giant asteroid is threatening to crash into their planet. The asteroid can be made from a giant crumpled mass of aluminum foil and brown tissue paper. Set the asteroid on top of an inverted wastepaper basket and place it at one end of the yard. Have players line up at the other end of the yard and take turns throwing "flying saucers" (Frisbees) at the asteroid. Each player gets 3 tries to "knock the asteroid off course" (off the wastepaper basket) and save his or her planet.

TIME MACHINE

Reports of cows being kidnapped by UFOs go back as far as the 1800s. Many people believe that aliens have been among us since the beginning of time. Their evidence of this is some of the man-made wonders of the world and their similarities—such as the Egyptian and Aztec pyramids. For this game you'll need a time machine. A large appliance box with a trap door will do just fine. It can be spray-painted silver and even decorated with colored flashing lights. On top of the time machine, place a ticking kitchen timer that can be set for 3-minute intervals. Players take turns getting into the time machine, 2 at a time. One player is the alien and the other player is a time traveler or "hostage from history."

While in the box the alien tells the time traveler who he or she is supposed to be, when and where he or she came from. The time traveler could be anyone from a caveman to King Arthur. After 3 minutes, the players emerge from the time machine to answer questions from the other players about the time and place they came from. The answers should be indirect, giving clues only. The first player who guesses who or where the time traveler is from gets to be the next alien and picks the next time traveler from the group. The game continues until everyone has been in the time machine.

PHOTO OPS

Be sure to have film that works in low light so that you can get shots of alien guests in the intergalactic conference room. Take photos of each alien wearing a planetary pendant, with his of her backwards name, and holding a custom-designed starship. These will make memorable keepsakes to send with thank-you notes.

 ## Goody Bags: Alien Convention Totes

Decorate black or midnight blue tote bags with stick-on silver stars and glitter (for the Milky Way). You can even use glitter paint to write something like **2001** (or whatever the year) **ALIEN CONVENTION** on the bag. Fill it with "alien novelties": alien bean bags, bracelets, erasers, magnets, stickers, or finger puppets. (Oriental Trading Company, 1-800-228-2269, is a great resource for extraterrestrial trinkets.) Some other ideas: World globe key chains (cut out paper keys and write strategic places on them like **THE WHITE HOUSE** or **NASA**), miniature flashlights for "laser beams," and soap bubble bottles relabeled **SPACE BUB-BLES.**

Extraterrestrial After-Dinner Mint Cake (recipe pages 111–113)

Personalized Pyramid Cakes
(recipe pages 129–130)

Recipes

UFO BAGEL BAR

Kids love to create their own sandwiches, and these really let the imagination run wild! Olives, pickles, and cellophane-frilled toothpicks make convincing lights and landing gear for bagel UFOs.

Ingredients:

12 bagels (these can be all the same or assorted flavors)
GARNISHES: pitted ripe olives, stuffed green olives, baby sweet gherkins, dill pickle slices, pretzel sticks, cellophane-frilled toothpicks
FILLINGS: sliced ham, bologna, turkey, cheese
CONDIMENTS: mayonnaise, mustard, softened butter, cream cheese
Makes 12 servings

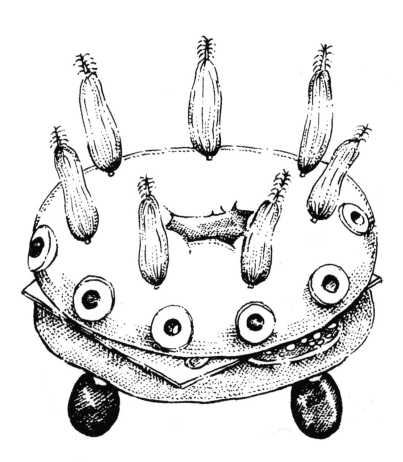

Directions:

1. Split bagels open so that they can be used as sandwiches.

2. Make one bagel UFO for kids to see as an example. Use toothpicks to attach olives or gherkins for landing gear (you could also use pretzel sticks). Olives and pickle slices also make effective lights and windows.

3. Arrange fillings on a platter and put condiments in dishes. Provide plenty of toothpicks for creative expression.

POD PEOPLE'S CHIPS AND RED PLANET DIP

Another popular theory about aliens is that they grow out of pods. That's the theme behind this menu item. Just add snow pea pods along with kid-favorite carrots, celery sticks, chips, and this traditional Martian dip to the UFO bagel buffet.

Ingredients:

2 8-oz. packages cream cheese, softened
3 Tbs. ketchup or chili sauce
1 tsp. Worcestershire sauce
1 16-oz. jar mild salsa
Makes 12 servings

Directions:

1. Beat cream cheese, ketchup (or chili sauce), and Worcestershire sauce until smooth.

2. Blend in salsa.

3. Cover and chill until serving time.

Dippers:

snow pea pods	potato chips
celery sticks	tortilla chips
carrot sticks	bagel or pita chips

EXTRATERRESTRIAL AFTER-DINNER MINT CAKE

This is any easy, make-from-a-mix cake with a little help from food coloring. After all, aliens are almost always green, both inside and out! Of course, if your kid is a die-hard chocolate lover, just use a chocolate cake mix.

Ingredients:

1 package white cake mix
1 tsp. peppermint extract
green paste food coloring
1 8-oz. bar dark, sweet chocolate
BUTTERMINT FROSTING (recipe
    follows)
$4^1/2$-oz. tube of chocolate deco-
    rating icing with round writing tip

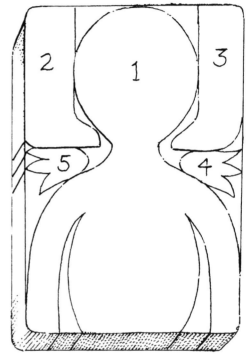

Fig. 1

Directions:

1. Preheat oven to 350°F (180°C). Prepare mix according to directions, adding peppermint extract and green food coloring to desired shade.

2. Chop chocolate into very small chunks and fold into batter.

3. Line a 9 x 13-inch pan with baking parchment. Spread batter in pan and bake 35 to 40 minutes.

4. Cool cake completely. Remove from pan by inverting onto baking sheet and peeling away paper.

5. Cover a 10 x 20-inch sheet of cardboard with foil.

6. Cut cake as shown in diagram (*Fig. 1*).

7. Arrange on board as shown (*Fig. 2*).

8. Cover cake evenly with frosting, smoothing with a metal spatula.

9. Use tube of chocolate decorating icing to pipe eyes, mouth, and "TAKE ME TO YOUR LEADER" on the cake or decorate with assorted candies (*Fig. 3*).

Fig. 2   Fig. 3

BUTTERMINT FROSTING

Ingredients:
$1/2$ cup unsalted butter, softened
$1/2$ cup shortening
4 cups powdered sugar
3 to 5 Tbs. milk
$1/2$ to 1 tsp. peppermint extract
green paste food coloring

Directions:

1. Cream butter and shortening together.

2. Beat in powdered sugar, adding enough milk to make frosting a smooth spreading consistency.

3. Add peppermint extract to taste and green food coloring to the desired shade.

FROZEN FLYING SAUCERS

This simple concoction of store-bought cookies, ice cream, and M&Ms makes very convincing vanilla or chocolate flying saucers. They're so much fun to make that you might want to let the aliens do it themselves.

Ingredients:

12 extra-large, packaged soft sugar cookies
1 can vanilla or milk chocolate frosting
M&Ms candies
1 quart vanilla or chocolate ice cream
   (use the same flavor of frosting and ice cream)
Makes 12 servings

Directions:

1. Use a metal spatula to spread frosting smoothly over cookies.

2. Decorate around edges of cookies with M&Ms (*Fig. 1*).

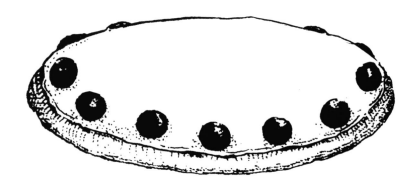

Fig. 1

3. Place a scoop of ice cream in center of each cookie and add a few more M&Ms for lights (*Fig. 2*).

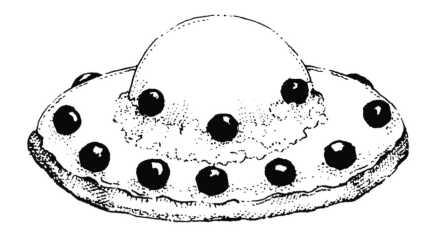

Fig. 2

ROCKET FUEL

Cover juice boxes with your own labels for "ROCKET FUEL" that feature an alien face on the front. On the back, write "FOR LIGHT YEARS OF LASTING ENERGY."

CLEOPATRA'S PYRAMID PARTY

(COULD ALSO BE CALLED QUEEN OF THE NILE PYRAMID PARTY)

GIRLS AGES 8 TO 12

The glamorous Cleopatra . . . the elegant Nefertiti . . . those queens of the Nile have intrigued generation after generation of young girls. These women—and the ancient culture they came from—had the ultimate sense of style. Who hasn't been captivated by images of the Great Pyramid, the Giant Sphinx, and the tomb of Tutankhamen? (When I was a child, I remember wrapping up my Ken doll in gauze followed by gold florist foil and then telling everyone he was "King Tut.") Our minds tend to lump all of these famous Egyptian symbols together into one big anachronism because it's so staggering to comprehend the actual time span of this great civilization. For example, the Great Pyramid was built 1,200 years before the reign of Tutankhamen and 2,500 years before Cleopatra—in other words, they were as ancient to her as she is to us! For the sake of entertainment, why not take some poetic license in the history department? This party appeals to

MENU

PHARAOH PHRANKS
WITH OSIRIS SAUCE

CHEOPS CHIPS
AND DIP

PERSONALIZED
PYRAMID CAKES

CLEOPATRA'S
CHOCOLATE ICE
CREAM CATS

NILE WATER

girls who are almost too old for theme parties. It combines all of our favorite classic Egyptian icons, regardless of whether they came from 3000 B.C. or 30 B.C.

Party Elements

Invitation: "Can't Read the Handwriting on the Wall?" Paper Pyramid with Rosetta Stone

Decorations: Front door mummy case, hieroglyphic balloons, color-in tomb paintings in the party room, sacred animal statues, pyramid place markers

Party Gear: Cleopatra's Collar

Instant Involvement: "Egyptician Salon"

Games/Activities: Jewelry Workshop, Walk Like an Egyptian, Mummy Wrap

Goody Bags: Sphinx Sacks

Invitation: Paper Pyramid with Rosetta Stone

Naturally, Cleopatra's Pyramid Party invitation is a paper pyramid—and you need the Rosetta Stone to actually read it.

Materials:

9 9 x 12-inch sheets light brown construction paper
1 9 x 12-inch sheet slate gray construction paper
ruler
scissors
assorted colored felt-tip markers or colored pencils (be sure you have black and brown)
12 photocopies of tomb art
12 7 x 9-inch envelopes

Directions:

1. For each invitation, fold a sheet of brown construction paper so that it measures 6 x 9 inches with the fold at the bottom.

2. Make a mark at the top midpoint and 1 inch from each edge along the bottom fold.

3. Use ruler as a straightedge to draw lines between marks (*Fig. 1*).

4. Cut along lines. You should have an equilateral triangle with 7-inch sides and the fold at the bottom (*Fig. 2*).

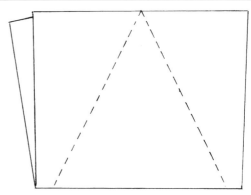

Fig. 1

5. On one side of pyramid, use a dark brown marker to make vertical and horizontal lines to score "stones" (*Fig. 3*). This will be the outside of the nvitation.

6. Cut out photocopies of tomb art (see pattern). Color in with markers or pencils.

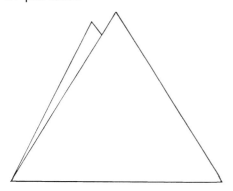

7. Open pyramid so that it looks like a diamond shape.

8. Paste tomb art in the area shown on the inside of the pyramid (*Fig. 4*).

9. In bottom triangle write in black: "Can't Read the Handwriting on the Wall?" (*Fig. 5*).

Fig. 2

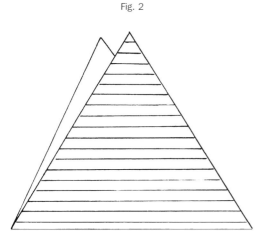

Fig. 3

Fig. 4

117

For Rosetta Stones (which go inside each invitation):

1. Cut construction paper into 3-inch squares.

2. Tear the edges at the top and bottom so that they're a little ragged and write "ROSETTA STONE" on one side (*Fig. 6*).

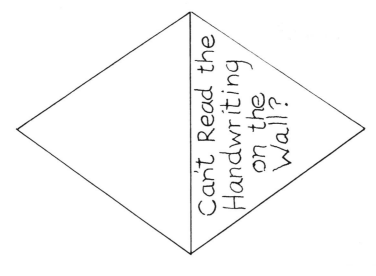

Fig. 5

Fig. 6

3. On the other side, write your invitation very small. (TIP: It can also be photocopied and pasted on one side.)

Inviting all Imaku (friends of the pharaoh)
Come to the Great Pyramid
to celebrate (your daughter's name)**'s birthday**
at (your address)
on (date) at (time)
RSVP (your phone number)

---

4. Insert a Rosetta Stone in each pyramid and place in envelopes.

NOTE: When guests RSVP, be sure to tell them about the "dress code." Ask them to wear sandals and bring a long (parent-size) white or off-white T-shirt to use as an Egyptian dress. King-size pillowcases also work well for this . . . as long as it's OK to cut arm and neck holes.

Decorations

For a smashing first impression, greet guests at the door with a life-size mummy case. As a guide for approximate size, have an adult lie down on a large slab of cardboard with arms folded in front. Loosely draw around the body, using a photo or illustration of a mummy case for reference. Paint to look like a mummy case and mount on the front door (*Fig. 1*). This is also a great activity to do after the kids arrive. Once inside the party room, line the walls

Fig. 1

Fig. 2

with plain brown wrapping paper that's been decorated with murals of hieroglyphics and tomb paintings (*Fig. 2*). Note: This can even be turned into a party activity. Draw the outline designs of the mural in black crayon or marker. Color in one wall as an example and let the kids finish the rest. Be sure not to use markers or any product that will bleed through the paper if the kids are going to color in the murals after they've been hung on your walls.

Partially fill balloons with air. Carefully draw hieroglyphics on balloons with markers. Completely inflate and hang around the room (*Fig. 3*).

Fig. 3

Drape the party table with a neutral linen cloth. The Egyptians used lots of baskets and pottery, so you'll want to do the same when setting the table. Fill baskets and bowls with fresh and dried fruits, nuts, and yogurt-coated almonds or raisins for snacking. You can make a sphinx centerpiece by crunching up heavy-duty aluminum foil to make a form and covering it with strips of papier mâché (*Fig. 4*). When dry, paint to look like the great Sphinx (*Fig. 5*).

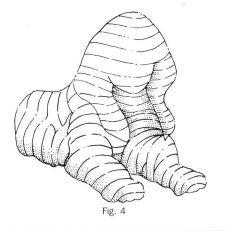

Fig. 4

Fig. 5

Certain animals were very prominent in Egyptian culture. Cats, for example, were considered sacred. Monkeys were captured for ladies' pets, and baboons were used as guard animals. The hippopotamus was hunted as part of a religious sacrifice. The Egyptians believed that the evil god Seth was hiding inside the body of a hippo. Archeologists have found statues of all these creatures in pyramids and tombs.

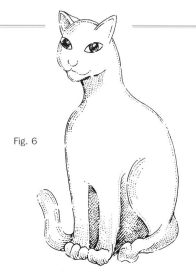

Fig. 6

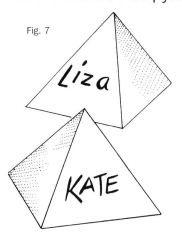

Fig. 7

You can make your own tomb statues out of cheap plastic or rubber toy animals. Simply spray-paint them with special-effect granite or marbleizing paints, which are available at paint and hardware stores (*Fig. 6*). To mark each guest's place setting, make individual 3-dimensional pyramids out of cardboard or construction paper. Write each guest's name on her pyramid (*Fig. 7*).

Party Gear: Cleopatra's Collar

Throughout the ages of Egyptian fashion, one of the most notable accessories was a dramatic, circular beaded collar. Semiprecious stones, glazed beads, and inlays were preferred. For costume purposes, these collars can be made out of black felt and enhanced with paint-on "gold and jewels." You can also glue on sequins, beads, or paste gems. Note: To estimate the amounts of paint, sequins, beads, or paste jewels you'll need, experiment on the first collar or two. When you come up with a design that pleases you, you'll know how much of each material you've used. Just be sure to make all of the collars very similar. The last thing you want is to have girls squabble over who got "the best one."

Materials:

$1^1/_4$ yds. 60-inch-wide black felt
pencil
sheet of newspaper (for pattern)
scissors
pins
decorative dimensional paints for fabric in writing tubes (choose a
    selection of pearl or glitter finish in colors like turquoise, emerald,
    and ruby, along with plenty of
    metallic gold and silver)
sequins, beads, or glue-on paste
    jewels and flexible fabric glue
    (Note: These are really optional.
    As a matter of economics, it's
    possible to make a collar com-
    pletely out of painted "jewels")
3 dozen black hooks and eyes
needle, black thread
Makes 12 collars

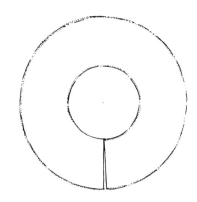

Fig. 1

Fig. 2

Directions:

1. Cut a 14-inch circle from a sheet of newspaper. Cut a 6-inch circle out of the center.

2. Cut circle open between neck hole and edge (*Fig. 1*). Use this as a pattern to cut 12 collars out of felt.

3. Use your imagination to decorate each collar with rows of gold bands alternating with zigzag and horizontally strung rows of "beads." If desired, add rows of glue-on sequins, beads, or paste jewels (*Fig. 2*).

4. Sew 3 sets of hooks and eyes on each side of collar openings (*Fig. 3*). Collars are fastened at the back of the neck.

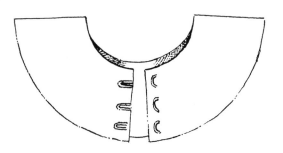

Fig. 3

Instant Involvement: "Egyptician Salon"

As soon as the girls arrive, usher them into the "Egyptician Salon." This ancient beauty spa is where they'll have a blast in the makeup and wardrobe department. For costumes, they'll try on their oversize T-shirts and turn them into tunics by either rolling up the sleeves or cutting them off. Offer them a selection of sashes, colored cord, or belts to use around their waists. To complete the look, present each with her "Cleopatra's Collar."

Have a makeup table set with gaudy green, blue, and even glittery gold eye shadow. You'll also need plenty of black eyeliner. (Note: you can use regular cosmetics or Halloween costume makeup.) Offer a selection of quick-drying metallic-finish nail enamel for girls to paint their fingers and toes. Among the amusing aspects of ancient hair care products are some of the ingredients: "gazelle dung, hippopotamus fat, and bull blood." The girls will really get a laugh out of using cans of hair spray and mousse relabeled as such. Girls this age also love to use spray-in, wash-out garish hair colors. Temporary tattoos and fingernail decals are also popular. Once the girls have completed their makeovers, it's time for the first game/activity: JEWELRY WORKSHOP.

 # Games/Activities

JEWELRY WORKSHOP

After being dressed for the role of Egyptian royalty, it will be hard to pull the girls away from this activity. Beaded headbands and arm bracelets were essential to a fashionable Egyptian wardrobe, and the girls will want to create their own designs. Set up an area where they can sit on the floor, surrounded by bowls and baskets of colored beads and strips of cord, yarn, or suede laces for stringing. If economy is an issue, you can make wonderful beads by spray-painting dry macaroni or other tube-shaped pasta in several different colors. To do this, you need to arrange the pasta on aluminum foil. Lightly spray one side. When dry, turn and spray the other side. Be sure the pasta has dried thoroughly before putting in baskets or bowls so that they won't stick together. Demonstrate with a sample of how beads can be strung to tie around as a headband and bracelets . . . then let the girls use their own imagination.

WALK LIKE AN EGYPTIAN

As one might imagine, body odor was a persistent problem in ancient times. Before the days of antiperspirants, men and women sprinkled their clothes with perfume made from myrrh, frankincense, and fragrant plants. On any given day in the Egyptian court, you could see ladies walking around with waxy cones on top of their heads. These were anointed with scented oils that were designed to melt in the hot sun—the idea being that, by the evening banquet, they'd still smell good!

This makes a great premise for a goofy game. For cones you can simply use inverted ice cream wafer cones or plastic cups. Have players line up side by side at one end of the yard or room. At the signal, the antics begin (a gong works well—or start playing the '80s recording of "Walk Like an Egyptian" or the '70s hit "King Tut"). Each player tries to balance an "anointed oil cone" on her head as she does an "Egyptian-style walk" (arms and legs mimicking the profile of a classic tomb painting). Each players "walks" to the opposite side of the yard or room and back. If the cone falls off, she has to freeze in whatever position she was walking in. If the cone stays balanced on top of her head, she turns right around and repeats the trip as soon as she reaches her starting position. The last player left moving wins. Best of all, everyone gets a big laugh watching each other look ridiculous.

MUMMY WRAP

This is an ancient Egyptian takeoff on the time-honored bridal shower ritual of making toilet paper gowns. For this game players use rolls of toilet paper to wrap each other up like mummies. Divide girls into pairs and provide each pair with two rolls of white toilet paper.

(Note: Some economy brands have become so skimpy that you might have to give each pair of players four rolls.) At the starting signal (use one of the suggestions from the previous game), one player wraps her partner completely in toilet paper, "mummy style." Once they've used up a complete roll of paper, the mummy has to be unwrapped, and it's the other partner's turn to be wrapped and unwrapped with the second roll of toilet paper. The first pair of players to complete the whole process wins.

PHOTO OPS

Take the opportunity to catch guests at particularly silly moments during the makeup session and the "Walk Like an Egyptian" and "Mummy Wrap" games. These will make timeless keepsakes to send with the thank-you notes.

 # Goody Bags: Sphinx Sacks

Decorate simple brown lunch bags with hieroglyphic designs, using a black calligraphy pen or brush point marker. Favor ideas: combs, mirrors, play makeup, sample or trial-size bottles of cologne or perfume, scented candles, play jewelry, and miniature jars of honey. Dried fruits, nuts, and Jordan almonds or yogurt-covered almonds can be wrapped in simple parchment bundles and tied with natural cord. Tie goody bags at the top with natural cord.

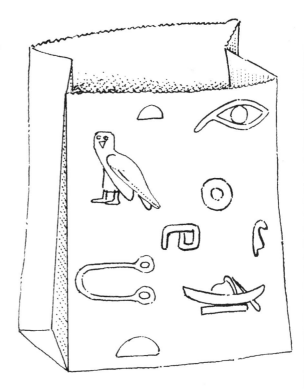

 **Recipes**

PHARAOH PHRANKS

These funny little franks look like a mummy case resting peacefully on the plate. This recipe allows one "phrank" per guest, but you can double the recipe for a group with a big appetite.

Ingredients:
12 beef, pork, or turkey franks
3 cans soft breadsticks
toothpicks
one egg beaten with 1 Tbs. water
6 ripe olives
OSIRIS SAUCE (recipe follows)
Makes 12 servings

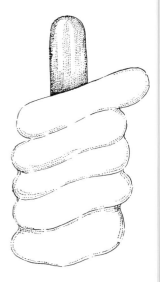

Fig. 1

Directions:

1. Preheat oven to 375°F (190°C). Cover 2 large baking sheets with baking parchment and spray lightly with nonstick cooking spray.

2. Open cans of breadsticks and separate into strips. (Note: These tend to get sticky and hard to handle when warm, so keep each can refrigerated until you're ready to use it.)

3. Starting at one end of each frank, wrap a breadstick around it, covering about three-quarters of it (*Fig. 1*).

4. Mold dough with hands so that the seams are pressed together, and flatten around the base where the mummy's feet would be (*Fig. 2*).

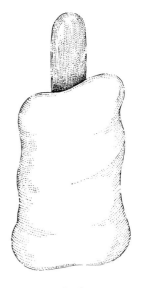

Fig. 2

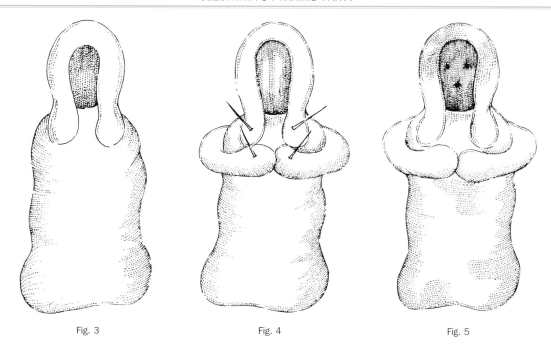

Fig. 3   Fig. 4   Fig. 5

5. Arrange about 3 inches apart on baking sheets. Use remaining breadsticks for hair and arms. For each frank, drape half a piece of breadstick around the "head" and down the front, like hair. Press securely in place (*Fig. 3*).

6. Mold arms and hands out of the other half breadstick, wrapping around the back of the frank and coming together in the front. Pinch dough to look like hand shapes (*Fig. 4*).

7. Brush with egg glaze. Anchor hair along sides of the head and hands with toothpicks while baking.

8. Bake 7 minutes and check. If hair or arms are puffing away from the body, remove baking sheet from oven and carefully press warm dough back into place. Bake an additional 7 to 10 minutes, or until golden brown.

9. Just before serving, shave off the outer layer of ripe olives to use for making facial features. Cut into small pieces for eyes and mouth.

10. To serve, remove toothpicks from the franks and garnish them with olive faces (*Fig. 5*). Serve with OSIRIS SAUCE.

TIME-SAVING TIP: Bake these a day in advance and reheat in a warm oven, loosely covered with foil. Add faces at the last minute.

OSIRIS SAUCE

Ingredients:
1 cup yellow mustard
$1/2$ cup mayonnaise (regular or reduced fat)
3 Tbs. honey
1 Tbs. orange juice concentrate

Directions:
Combine all ingredients in a small bowl or glass measuring cup and blend with a wire whisk or fork. Keep chilled until serving time.

CHEOPS CHIPS AND DIP

Olives were an important staple in the ancient Egyptian diet. So why not serve pyramid-shaped pita or tortilla chips with olive dip?

Ingredients:
1 8-oz. package cream cheese (regular, reduced
    fat, or fat-free), softened
1 8-oz. carton sour cream (regular, reduced fat,
    or fat-free)
$1/2$ tsp. celery salt
3 Tbs. snipped fresh chives
$1/2$ cup chopped ripe olives or green olives (your
    child's preference), or use $1/2$ cup grated cheddar
    cheese (if your child's not an olive fan)
pita chips; flour or corn tortilla chips (or offer a selection
    of all three in a basket)
Makes 12 servings

Directions:
1. Whip cheese until soft and smooth.

2. Blend in sour cream, celery salt, and chives.

3. Stir in olives (or cheese). Cover and chill.

4. Serve dip in the center of the basket surrounded by chips all carefully positioned upright to resemble pyramids.

PERSONALIZED PYRAMID CAKES

Just like the pyramids of Giza, these cakes "rise from the desert sand," only they're on a desert of brown sugar. Each girl gets to decorate her own according to her personal taste. You'll probably have a lot of leftover cake scraps after you've sculpted the pyramids. Not to worry . . . these usually disappear faster than a leftover can of frosting.

Ingredients:

3 packages (10³/4-oz. each)
   frozen pound cake
cans of assorted frosting flavors
   (vanilla, lemon, strawberry, and
   chocolate)
cake decorations (M&Ms, redhots,
   sprinkles, nonpareils, licorice
   strings . . .
light brown sugar
Makes 12 servings

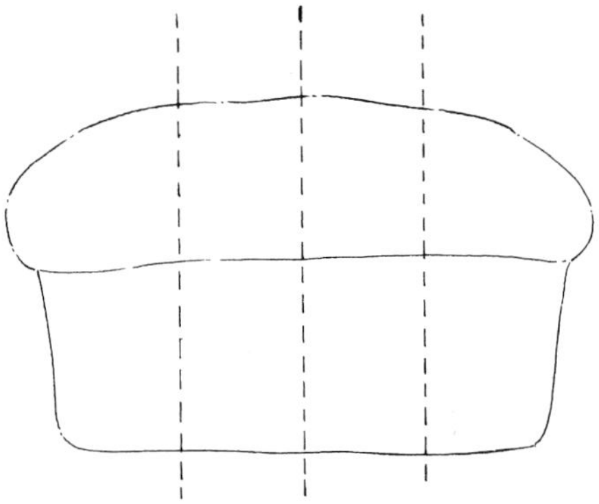

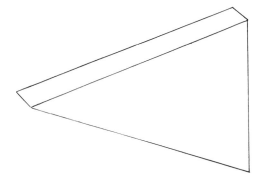

Fig. 1

Directions:

1. Partially defrost pound cakes. Cut each loaf into quarters (*Fig. 1*).

2. Trim pieces into triangular wedges (*Fig. 2*).

3. Trim wedges into pyramids (*Fig. 3*). Chill again so that they'll be easier to frost.

4. Arrange cans of frosting and bowls of decorations around the table. (Note: You might want to divide the contents of each can into several dishes so that it circulates around the group.) Provide plastic knives for spreading.

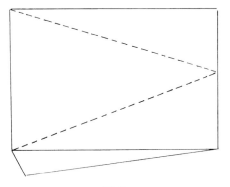

Fig. 2

Fig. 3

5. Place each cake on a paper or plastic dessert plate and surround with brown sugar "sand." Present to each Egyptian princess for her personal touch.

POUND CAKE SCRAPS? Here's an idea: Make an "unbirthday" trifle. Layer scraps of cake in a bowl and cover with jam and fresh fruit. Top with your child's favorite flavor of pudding and whipped cream. Serve after a day or two, when the post-birthday blues set in.

CLEOPATRA'S CHOCOLATE ICE CREAM CATS

Worshiped as sacred animals, cats were popular pets among the ancient Egyptians. Classic cat statues that once adorned their tombs are now famous museum pieces. These chocolate ice cream cats are an easy treat to whip up . . . so easy, in fact, that you might want to let the party guests have the fun of making their own.

Ingredients:
1 gallon chocolate fudge (dark chocolate) ice cream
24 small green gumdrops
24 large black gumdrops
toothpicks
1 16-oz. can chocolate fudge frosting
large ice cream scoop (#20 food scoop)
small ice cream scoop (#100 food scoop)
pastry bag with coupling nozzle and
   #2 or #4 round writing tip
Makes 12 servings

Directions:

1. Cover a tray with aluminum foil.

2. Place 12 large scoops of ice cream on the foil.

3. Push a small scoop of ice cream into the side of each large scoop (*Fig. 1*).

4. Flatten green and black gumdrops with a rolling pin.

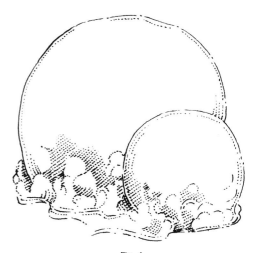

Fig. 1

5. Cut green gumdrops into oval shapes for eyes and black gumdrops into the shape of cats' ears (*Fig. 2*).

6. Press eyes onto the large scoop and attach ears, using toothpicks if necessary.

7. Fill pastry bag with fudge frosting and outline gumdrops for dramatic eyes. Pipe pupils on eyes; add nose and mouth (*Fig. 3*). Return to freezer for at least 3 hours before serving.

Fig. 3

Fig. 2

NILE WATER

The Nile River is not known for being a beautiful shade of Caribbean blue or sea green. A humorous way to play with this idea is to serve "Nile Water" for beverages. All you have to do is serve cream soda, root beer, or iced tea in cups decorated with the words NILE WATER. You can also put fake labels on soda cans.

THE STAR AWARDS

AGES 9 TO 12

The entertainment world pats itself on the back with annual, never-ending awards ceremonies. The Oscars, Emmys, Tonys, and Grammys honor the best and brightest in their industries. But what about those films that flop, sitcoms that fade after four episodes, plays that fold when the curtain closes on opening night, and one-hit wonders that fall off the pop charts like lead? Just for a change, wouldn't it be fun to celebrate mediocre media (the way so much of it really is) with a parody awards party. Kids love doing send-ups and spoofs of their favorite (and not so favorite) music, TV, and film stars. "The Star Awards" gives them the opportunity to play producer, writer, singer, and actor at a skill level they can easily accomplish. By including every genre of entertainment, this party will appeal to each and every guest.

 Party Elements

Invitation: Television Guide

Decorations: Searchlights, Hollywood Walk of Fame, backstage entrance sign, Wall of Fame, pop star posters, movie magazine mats, CD plates, and Star Awards

Party Gear: Glamour Glasses

Instant Involvement: Tinseltown Tabloid

MENU

HOLLYWOOD WRAPS

CALIFORNIA
CUCUMBER DIP
AND CHIPS

STAR-STUDDED SALAD

BEVERLY HILLS
HOT TUB CAKE

WORLD PREMIERE
FROZEN BONBONS

DOM PERIN "POP"

Games/Activities: Worst Screenplay, Worst Sitcom, Worst Hit Single
Goody Bags: Popcorn Bags

Invitation: Television Guide

For this invitation, you'll need to plan ahead by saving your old weekly television magazines or collecting castoffs from friends and neighbors. You can also use the television guides that come in the Sunday paper.

Materials:
12 television guides or weekly television magazines
craft knife
ruler, pencil, scissors
stapler
photocopies or computer printouts of invitation (as follows)
envelopes to fit guides
Makes 12 invitations

Directions:

1. Use craft knife to carefully cut the front and back covers off of the guides. Also cut out the table of contents, horoscope, reviews, or any other section you want to include in the invitation.

2. Design your invitation message so that it will fit the size of one of the pages. Because you're using old guides that have different cover dates, write up the invitation as a coming attraction (not necessarily for that week).

COMING ON (date of the party)
THE —th ANNUAL
(use the age of your child for the year)
STAR AWARDS

BROADCAST LIVE FROM
(your address)
AT (time of party)

Since this won't take up the entire 8^1/$_2$ x 11-inch sheet of paper, use the remaining space on the page to make a "backstage pass":

OFFICIAL BACKSTAGE PASS FOR THE —th ANNUAL STAR AWARDS
PRESENT AT THE DOOR UPON YOUR ARRIVAL.
PROPER ATTIRE REQUESTED
RS-"VIP" (Your phone number)

---

3. Print up enough copies for your invitations.

4. Cut out the page to fit, and include a separate backstage pass for each guide.

5. Sandwich the invitation page right after the table of contents and before any of the other pages you are including, between the front and back covers.

6. Staple pages together within ^{1}/$_4$ inch of the left-hand margin.

7. Tuck a backstage pass inside each cover and enclose invitations in envelopes.

8. When guests RS-"VIP," tell them to come dressed as their favorite celebrity in the entertainment industry.

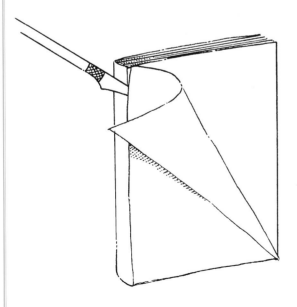
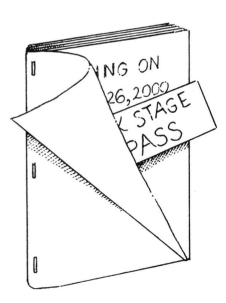

Decorations

Fig. 1

Make a sign across the garage door to be seen from the street that says: WELCOME TO THE 9th ANNUAL STAR AWARDS— assuming, for example, that your child is 9 (*Fig. 1*). If the party is held in the afternoon or evening, large flashlights or floodlights make great "searchlights." Use sidewalk chalk to create a "Hollywood Walk of Fame" on your

Fig. 2

driveway or front walk. Draw a sidewalk square with a star and a name inside it for each guest (*Fig. 2*). When guests arrive, this will be part of the TINSELTOWN TABLOID instant involvement activity. Put a sign on the front door that says BACK-STAGE ENTRANCE: VIP PASS REQUIRED (*Fig. 3*). Put up a "Wall of Fame" inside, where the stars can autograph a paper-lined wall. For fun, get the autographs started by writing other celebrity signatures on the wall before the kids arrive. (Note: Children will want to impersonate their contemporary idols. To avoid having guests arrive and already finding their name on the wall, you might want to write famous names from another gener-ation like Frank Sinatra, Marilyn Monroe, Jimmy Stewart. . . .) Line the walls of the party room with pop star posters. Hang CDs from the ceiling. You can make "Movie Magazine Place Mats" by cutting out a collage of photographs from the pages of tabloid magazines.

Fig. 3

Fig. 4

Decoupage them to heavy cardboard using a liquid polymer and a craft painting sponge (*Fig. 4*). Buy silver paper or plastic plates for the meal or dessert. Use laundry markers to draw CD labels in the center for your child's favorite hit songs. For place markers, put an envelope on each plate that says: AND THE WINNER IS . . . (*Fig. 5*). Inside you can write the name of the guest. At first this may create some confusion, but that's part of the fun. Kids scramble around opening envelopes and looking for the right place to sit. Of course, be fully prepared for these stars to deny their original names before their agents had them changed to the ones the world is familiar with. Last but not least, you'll want to decorate the table with STAR AWARDS. Take a tip from those other award shows . . . just about any ridiculous-looking object could be a candidate. My personal favorite is to collect empty Mrs. Butterworth's maple syrup bottles and spray-paint them gold or silver (*Fig. 6*).

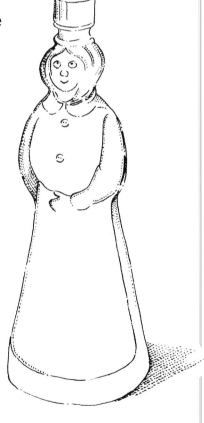

Fig. 5

Fig. 6

Party Gear: Glamour Glasses

Both you and your child will have fun making these fab star-style shades. In fact, you might want to include this as an activity and let the guests make their own.

Materials:
12 pairs of inexpensive sunglasses (these are easy to find at party supply stores)
craft glue
fine craft brush(es)
glitter (gold, silver, or an assortment of colors)
Makes 12 glasses

Directions:
While working on these remember to keep the glue off the lens! Otherwise you'll have either blurry smudges or glitter or both blocking the view.

1. Hold each pair of glasses by the ear tips. Carefully brush a light layer of glue along the outside of the frame, taking care not to touch the lens.

2. Hold glasses over a sheet of paper and sprinkle glitter over the frame.

3. Tap excess glitter off the glasses and onto the paper. Reuse the excess glitter.

4. Allow glasses to dry.

 # Instant Involvement: Tinseltown Tabloid

This turns the first "icebreaking" activity of the party into an opening night extravaganza. You'll need at least one gossip columnist and paparazzi. I suggest recruiting neighbors, older siblings, or parents for these jobs. As soon as each star arrives, there should be an onslaught of flashing cameras. (These photos will be used in the

"Tinseltown Tabloid.") Use several cameras. Not all of them have to have film, but of the ones that do, one should be Polaroid or a videocamera so that kids can see the pictures at the party. The gossip columnist sticks a tape recorder microphone (or a mock microphone) in the face of each arriving celeb, annoying them with questions about their relationships, career, denying reports of plastic surgery, etc. (Note: If the gossip columnist isn't taping these interviews with a real tape recorder, she'd better be taking notes.)

Once the celebrity guests have been interviewed, they find their square on the "Hollywood Walk of Fame." The stars use sidewalk chalk to sign their "stage name" next to their humble, little-known, pre-fame name. Because you won't have real cement to make hand and foot impressions, let the stars outline their shoes or hands with chalk. Of course, the paparazzi take more pictures of this performance. Later on you can set out the Polaroids or play the video at the party for the guests to watch. The photos and interview will be used later to make a tabloid-style thank-you letter to send to the guests. (See *PHOTO OPS*.)

 # Games/Activities

NOTE: You may not have time for all of the games. If not, choose just one.

WORST SCREENPLAY

This is a game where hopeful screenwriters are trying to pitch their first script to a famous Hollywood film producer. The game begins by having each player write a list of four well-known (or not so well-known) actors and another list of four characters to be played by the actors. Tell the writers that they can let their imaginations run wild in creating these roles—the more wacky or outrageous, the more fun. The lists are then wadded up into paper balls. You'll need two wastepaper baskets: All of the actor lists are tossed into one basket, and the character lists into the other. Each writer takes turns salvaging an actor list and a character list from the trash. Staple together a few sheets of writing paper between two sheets of light blue paper with the word

"SCREENPLAY" on the cover. Pass one out to each writer and give them a few minutes to come up with a "high concept" plot for their future film that uses their list of actors matched to their list of characters. After everyone's written down their plot, it's time to sell the producer on it.

Have the players sit in a circle around a director's chair. Put sunglasses on a big teddy bear and put him in the chair. Players take turns reading their plots to the producer and pitching (or pleading!) why this would make a hit movie. When they're finished, the rest of the players cast their vote by either applauding or holding their nose. In keeping with the tradition of the "STAR AWARDS," the film that really stinks . . . WINS!

WORST SITCOM

For this game, you'll want to use your video camera. Divide guests into two groups and tell each group that they are to play a scene based on their favorite sitcom. Let each group go into a huddle and decide what show to spoof and who plays what character. There's no need for a script; characters just ad lib, making up the dialogue as they go. Set up an area for the "sound stage." Since most sitcoms take place in ordinary rooms, any room will do. Each group gets a chance to perform in front of the other group and the camcorder. Announce "LIGHTS, CAMERA, ACTION!" and the scene begins. If the skit rambles on too long or the players get stuck, just call "CUT!" Meanwhile, the group playing audience also plays critic. They can vote to have the show canceled or renewed. Chances are it will be canceled . . . making it an ideal candidate for a "STAR AWARD"!

WORST HIT SINGLE

When guests "RS-VIP," tell them to bring their favorite (or least favorite) CD. Have players take turns lip-synching to their song in front of the awards-night panel of judges (the rest of the players). Thumbs up and it's a hit. . . . Thumbs down and it's a flop. Not to worry; dropping off the charts always guarantees entry into the "STAR AWARD HALL OF FAME."

PHOTO OPS

Remember those paparazzi picts that were taken at the "backstage door"? Come thank-you note time, use them with the interviews to put together a newsletter called the "Tinseltown Tabloid." It can cover all of the latest gossip, fashion faux pas, and reviews of the award-winning performances. Even if you don't have a computer with desktop publishing software, this is still a lot of fun (and educational) to do the old-fashioned way: cut, paste, and photocopy.

 # Goody Bags: Popcorn Bags

In keeping with the movie theme, look in party shops for cabana-striped paper tote bags that look like movie theater popcorn bags. Line them with tissue and throw in sample bottles of inexpensive perfumes, colognes, shampoos, moisturizers, and so on. (Travel bottles and freebies from hotels can be used for this.) Scarves or costume jewelry in mock Tiffany boxes or toy watches in faux Rolex boxes are great fun, as are key chains with fobs for luxury cars. (You can buy them or make your own out of cardboard.) For snacks, throw in a small box with one or two gourmet chocolates or truffles.

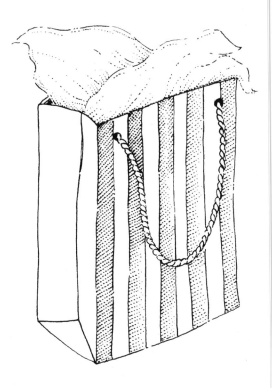

Don't forget to include a "Map to the Stars' Homes." Make one by photocopying a map of your neighborhood and marking the homes of your guests with their "pre-fame" names.

Star-Studded Salad
(recipe pages 142–143)

Chicken Kabobs with
Barbados Barbecue Sauce
(recipe pages 154–155)

 # Recipes

HOLLYWOOD WRAPS

These sandwiches are just the sort of snack you'd find waiting for the cast after a Hollywood-style "wrap party." All of the trendsetters at THE STAR AWARDS will think these colorful tortilla treats are "très trendy." You can make them up ahead of time or let the guests make their own from a wrap sandwich bar.

Ingredients:

12 8-inch spinach (or garden vegetable) flour tortillas
12 8-inch sun-dried tomato flour tortillas
whipped cream cheese with chives
guacamole
shredded romaine lettuce
chopped ripe olives
grated cheddar cheese
diced tomatoes (well drained)
thinly sliced smoked turkey
crisp crumbled bacon, turkey bacon, or imitation bacon bits
Makes 12 servings

Directions:

1. Spread spinach tortillas with softened cream cheese and sun-dried tomato tortillas with guacamole.

2. Top both types of tortillas with lettuce.

3. Sprinkle spinach tortillas with chopped olives and sun-dried tomato tortillas with cheddar cheese and chopped tomatoes.

4. Arrange thin slices of turkey over the olives and roll up. Sprinkle bacon over tomatoes and roll up.

5. Slice wrap sandwiches diagonally. Arrange on a large platter and serve. Alternatively, put all of the "fixings" out in dishes on a table or buffet and let the kids create their own.

CALIFORNIA CUCUMBER DIP AND CHIPS

Potato chips are a prerequisite at most kids' parties, no matter how sophisticated the soiree.

Ingredients:

1 pint sour cream (regular or reduced fat)
$1/2$ cup seeded minced cucumber
1 Tbs. chopped fresh dillweed (or 2 tsp. dried)
1 tsp. Worcestershire sauce
ruffled potato chips
Makes 12 servings

Directions:

1. Combine sour cream, cucumber, dill, and Worcestershire sauce.

2. Cover dip and refrigerate until serving time to blend flavors. Serve with chips.

STAR-STUDDED SALAD

Slices of the novel-looking carambola, or star fruit, resemble beautiful stars. Look for them in the specialty produce section of your supermarket (where they usually keep the kiwis and coconuts). If you can't find any in your area, garnish the salad with strawberry slices, arranged in star formations (five slices to form a star).

Ingredients:

1 ripe cantaloupe, cut into melon balls
1 ripe honeydew, cut into melon balls
4 cups pineapple chunks
1 8-oz. carton lemon yogurt
2 Tbs. mayonnaise (regular, reduced fat, or fat-free)
red leaf lettuce for garnish (outer leaves)
2–3 carambola fruit or 1 pint fresh strawberries
Makes 12 servings

Directions:

1. Combine cantaloupe, honeydew, and pineapple chunks in a large mixing bowl.

2. Blend lemon yogurt and mayonnaise together. Toss with fruit.

3. Line a large salad bowl with lettuce leaves and fill with fruit salad.

4. Slice carambola and arrange "stars" on top of salad or, to make strawberry stars, stem strawberries and split in half lengthwise. Arrange in clusters of 5 slices with tips pointing out like star points.

BEVERLY HILLS HOT TUB CAKE

Pretzels surround this cake like a cedar-sided spa hot tub. If you want to turn it into a swimming pool, just add a diving board. Either way, you can always invite a Barbie doll to just "hang out and make the Hollywood scene." Using a mix and canned frosting is extra convenient and gives you more time to build the hot tub.

Ingredients:

1 box cake mix (your child's favorite flavor)
2 16-oz. cans vanilla frosting
blue food coloring
thin pretzel rods
For pool: shortbread cookie, 2 small pieces of black shoestring
    licorice laces, giant gum balls or jawbreakers
Makes 12 servings

Directions:

1. Preheat oven and prepare batter according to directions on box.

2. Pour batter into a 10-inch springform pan lined with baking parchment. Bake until cake tests done.

3. Cool cake completely. Run a knife around sides of cake and release springform side.

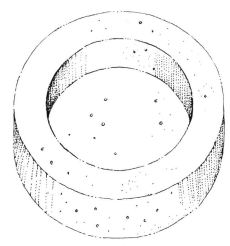

Fig. 1

4. Gently remove parchment paper from under cake and place cake on a 12-inch platter or cake board.

5. Using a small knife, cut a circular well in center of cake, leaving sides and bottom $1^1/2$ inches thick (*Fig. 1*).

6. Carefully remove center from the cake.

7. Tint 1 can of frosting blue. Spread blue frosting around inside walls and bottom of pool.

8. Spread top and outer sides of cake with white frosting.

9. Surround cake with pretzel rods, laying them close together so that they resemble wood siding.

If you're making a pool, put a shortbread cookie on top for a diving board and use the shoestring licorice laces to make rails. Add gum balls or jawbreakers for beach balls (*Fig. 2*).

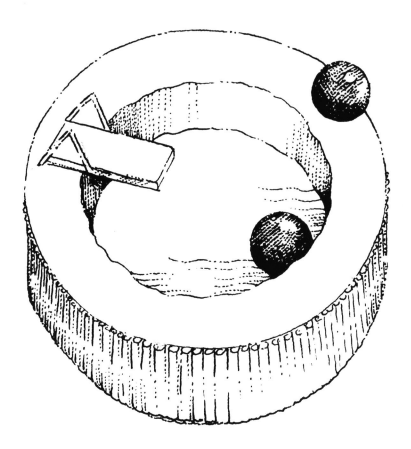

Fig. 2

WORLD PREMIERE FROZEN BONBONS

What's the brightest point of even the dullest movie? Going to the concession stand, of course, to buy outrageously overpriced popcorn and soda. My personal, all-time favorite is picking up a box of frozen ice cream bonbons. Now you can buy "shell-making" ice cream toppings at the supermarket. I like to use cherry ice cream because the end result resembles a chocolate-covered cherry cordial candy. Pecan praline, coffee, toffee, and chocolate mint ice creams also make delectable frozen confections.

Ingredients:

2 quarts ice cream in different flavors
3 to 4 bottles Magic Shell® ice cream topping
Makes 12 servings

Directions:

1. Line a couple of baking sheets with foil.

2. Using a miniature ice cream scoop (a #100 food scoop makes $1/2$-oz. to $3/4$-oz. balls), scoop ice cream balls onto foil and return to the freezer for a couple of hours, or until very firm.

3. Work with a few ice cream balls at a time, keeping the rest in the freezer. Hold each ball on a fork over a small, narrow bowl. Squeeze an even stream of topping over each ball, trying to coat it as evenly as possible, without wasting too much topping. Allow the excess to drip off. (If excess topping becomes too thick to reuse, you can soften it over a bowl of hot water.)

4. Immediately place coated balls on a clean sheet of foil and return to the freezer until serving time.

DOM PERIN "POP"

For this gala event, kids will feel like very grown-up superstars if you serve them ginger ale in plastic Champagne glasses. For that extra touch of class, serve a strawberry in each glass.

CARIBBEAN CRUISE PARTY

AGES 9 TO 11

Imagine a slumber party that sets sail at sunset, docks at exotic ports of call, and offers all the amenities of an ocean liner! This dream cruise brings a whole new level of fantasy-filled fun to the typical pizza and pajamas sleepover. With just a few decorations, it's easy to make believe that your home is a floating resort. If you need brochures, posters, and so on, just ask your local travel agent. I find they're more than happy to help. After all, these materials help promote real-life cruises to the party guests' parents.

 **Party Elements**

Invitation: Cruise Brochure with Boarding Passes

Decorations: Ship signs, life preservers, portholes, lounge chairs, travel posters, Captain's table, staterooms

Party Gear: Cruiseline Sunhats

Instant Involvement: Sun Deck Spa

Games/Activities: Ports of Call Shopping Spree, Souvenir Show-and-Tell

Goody Bags: Cruiseline Caddy

 MENU

CHICKEN KABOBS
WITH BARBADOS
BARBECUE SAUCE

MONTEGO BAY
MANGO SALAD

CRUISE SHIP CAKE

ICE CREAM LIFE
PRESERVERS

MOCK CHAMPAGNE
IN ICE BUCKETS

CRUISELINE
CONTINENTAL
BREAKFAST

Invitation: Cruise Brochure with Boarding Passes

All you really need to create this invitation is to visit your local travel agent. Or you can call cruiselines directly and tell them that you need 12 brochures. Either way, once you have the brochures all you have to do is make up boarding passes on a computer or word processor with the specifics of your party.

Materials:

12 brochures from a cruiseline of your choice
boarding passes (make on computer as described)
scissors or paper cutter
letter size envelopes
crayons or markers for decorating envelopes
Makes 12 invitations

Directions:

1. Cut boarding passes apart with scissors or paper cutter; there will be 3 to each $8^1/_2$ x 11-inch sheet.

2. Tuck them inside the brochure and enclose in envelopes.

3. Decorate the envelopes with enticing tropical motifs like palm trees, seashells, sunglasses, etc.

FOR BOARDING PASSES: Each pass will be one-third of a sheet of paper on your invitation so the print should be designed to fit in about a $3^1/_2$ x $8^1/_2$-inch space. For fun, the name of the ship should be the same as your daughter's (S.S. ALISON). For example, a boarding pass for a May 13th birthday/slumber party beginning at 6:00 P.M. with pick-up at noon the following morning might be something like this:

**(NAME OF CRUISELINE IN BROCHURE) 18-HOUR
WHIRLWIND CARIBBEAN TOUR
SHIP: S.S.** (your daughter's name)
BOARDING PASS: FIRST CLASS PASSENGER (name of invited guest)
DEPARTS FROM PORT (your address) on May 13 at 6:00 P.M.
RETURNS TO PORT (your address) on May 14 at 12:00 P.M.
**CONTACT CRUISE DIRECTOR FOR FURTHER
TRAVEL INFORMATION** (your phone number)

For authentic results, print your invitations on pastel-colored card stock. When guests call you (the cruise director) to RSVP, tell them to wear casual resort wear, pack a swimsuit, swim coverup, or terry robe, and something formal to wear to dinner at "the Captain's table."

Decorations

Think of your neighborhood as a harbor and make a sign to guide the arriving passengers to the ship. For example, if your neighborhood is named Westwood, you could make a sign pointing down your street that says WESTWOOD HARBOR AHEAD. Post a sign with a cruise liner on it at the end of the drive, pointing toward the "dock" (house). Rope off a walkway leading to the front door once the passengers have reached the dock. Because this is a slumber party, the so-called party room tends to take over the entire house. For that reason, you may want to decorate several rooms. For example, cover the walls of one room with travel posters. In the room where the girls will be sleeping, you can put up a sign like FIRST CLASS PASSENGER STATEROOMS, and then put portholes on the walls. Your patio, deck, or even the basement

can be transformed into a sun deck with lounge chairs. Use sidewalk chalk or tape to make a shuffleboard court and use tuna or pet food cans for shuffleboard disks. Don't forget to hang life preservers around the ship with the name of your ship: S.S. (your daughter's name). Use actual inflatable life preservers or Styrofoam rings. Finally, the cruiseline's dining room will be the scene for dinner at the Captain's table. Set it with a white tablecloth and silver or gold (plastic) flatware. Decorate the plates with nontoxic crayons or markers, using the cruiseline's logo.

Party Gear: Cruiseline Sunhats

This is a simple project that can even be made by the "passengers" as an entertaining activity. Party supply shops and catalogs have very reasonable prices on straw hats or canvas hats. In fact, they're cheaper by the dozen and often sold in sets of 12.

Materials:
12 straw or canvas hats with a brim
dimensional paint in writing tube
(if using canvas hats you can also use puff paint, for texture)

Directions:
As you now know from making invitations and decorating for this party, the cruise ship is named after your daughter. So, if your daughter's name is Melissa, the hats should all say: S.S. MELISSA. Depending on the style of the hat, the letters can either go around the crown or the brim (*Fig. 1*). Canvas-style hats can even have the letters painted under the brim, and turned up like a sailor's hat (*Fig. 2*). Follow the manufacturer's directions for the paint and allow to dry thoroughly before wearing.

Fig. 1

Fig. 2

Instant Involvement: Sun Deck Spa

A cruise is like a floating resort and part of being a pampered passenger is getting the spa treatment. As soon as the girls arrive, have them check into their stateroom, unpack their luggage and change into their swimsuits, swim coverups, or terry robes. Designate your deck, patio, porch, or even your basement (if it's winter or raining) as the ship's sun deck. Set out folding lounge chairs (borrow extras from friends and neighbors, if needed). Pass out thick towels, play music, and serve tropical-looking punch drinks with fruit and umbrella garnishes. As part of the spa treatment, let the girls give each other mud pack facials, cucumber eye treatments, manicures, and pedicures. Turn a wading pool into a jacuzzi with a garden hose. You can even provide sunless tanning lotion for those who want to return home looking like they actually went on a real cruise.

 # Games/Activities

PORTS OF CALL SHOPPING SPREE

To some people, the best part of a cruise is when they can get off the boat and go SHOPPING! With this in mind, the Caribbean thrives on tourists bringing back all sorts of collectibles and curios. Of course, nothing is ever for sale at the sticker price. As a child, we went on a vacation to Jamaica. I remember making several trips to the straw market where we bartered for everything from baskets to bongo drums. One of the merchants' favorite phrases was "Money is no problem, man." For this game, you'll need to divide the passengers into two shopping groups. Each group gets to take turns playing the role of shoppers and merchants. Set up two straw markets in ports on different Caribbean islands. These can be anywhere from Barbados to St. Bart's. Because you're dividing the passengers into two groups, there should be enough merchandise in each straw market for everyone to have something to buy. Suppose you have 12 players—6 shoppers and

6 merchants. Give each shopper the same amount of play money. (It doesn't matter if it's one dollar or one hundred dollar bills, give each player 5 bills so that she will have more to bargain with.) At the first port, each merchant sits in the stall (or table) with her merchandise in front of her. Each shopper must buy something and negotiate the price with the merchant.

Everything must be sold. The shopper who gets the best bargain wins (pays the least for her merchandise), and the merchant who makes the most profit wins. At the next straw market, in the next port of call, on the next island, the roles are reversed. This time the merchants get to be shoppers and vice-versa.

SOUVENIR SHOW-AND-TELL

This can be played before or after dinner at the Captain's table. It's really the conclusion of the previous game. Just like Show-and-Tell, passengers make up a story involving the souvenir they bought in the port of call that day. It could include anything they can dream up about that day's adventure (such as fighting over buying it with a famous celebrity or nearly losing it overboard to a swarm of sharks). The more ridiculous the tale, the more fun.

PHOTO OPS

For funny photos, try getting candid shots of the girls at the "Sun Deck Spa" with towels wrapped around their heads, mud packs on their faces, and cucumbers over their eyes. Some real-life cruises have a photographer circulating around the dining room taking keepsake photos of dinner guests. You can do the same when the girls are dressed up for dinner at the Captain's table.

Goody Bags: Cruiseline Caddy

Paint the name of the ship on canvas tote bags. (I've found that these are very inexpensive if purchased through paper/party supply outlets.) Fill them with all sorts of travel- or trial-size samples of personal care products: shampoo, moisturizer, sunscreen, brush, comb, and mini hand mirrors. A toy ship, gourmet chocolate mints (like the kind fine hotels but on your pillows at night), and a hand towel with the name of the ship embroidered on it (with a simple chain stitch) are also authentic touches.

 **Recipes**

CHICKEN KABOBS WITH BARBADOS BARBECUE SAUCE

When you're entertaining a houseful of girls for an overnight, you want to keep the menu preparation simple. This menu is fairly easy, using ready-made chicken nuggets. Giving a fancy flair to the kid-friendly classic will make the banquet at the Captain's table seem all the more elegant.

Ingredients:

Frozen chicken nuggets (allow 6 pieces per kabob)
1 large, fresh pineapple (or canned pineapple chunks)
24 cherry tomatoes
12 wooden kabob skewers
$1/2$ cup warm honey
BARBADOS BARBECUE SAUCE (recipe follows)
Makes 12 servings

Directions:

1. Core pineapple and cut into $3/4$-inch slices, leaving skin on.

2. Slice into wedgelike chunks.

3. Arrange chunks in a baking dish between thick layers of paper towels, to drain off extra moisture, and refrigerate pineapple overnight.

4. Bake chicken nuggets according to package directions.

5. Thread 6 chicken nuggets onto skewers, alternating with pineapple chunks and a cherry tomato on each end.

6. Place kabobs on a foil-lined baking sheet and brush pineapple chunks with honey.

7. Reheat in a 350°F (180°C) oven for about 5 or 6 minutes before serving. For a tropical touch, serve the barbecue sauce in seashells or hollowed-out orange skins, left over from squeezing fresh orange juice.

BARBADOS BARBECUE SAUCE

Ingredients:

1 12-oz. bottle of chili sauce
1 12-oz. jar of apricot preserves
$1/2$ tsp. ginger
3 Tbs. lime juice
3 Tbs. honey
1–2 tsp. mesquite smoke flavoring
    (optional)

Directions:

Combine ingredients in a small saucepan and bring to a boil.
Simmer for 3 minutes.

MONTEGO BAY MANGO SALAD

Major Grey's mango chutney is the secret ingredient in this zesty
spinach salad.

Ingredients:

$1/2$ cup Major Grey's mango chutney
$1/4$ cup honey
$1/4$ cup red wine vinegar
$1/2$ tsp. dry mustard
$1/2$ tsp. salt
$1/2$ tsp. Worcestershire sauce
1 cup vegetable oil
3 10-oz. packages fresh, washed spinach
1 lb. crisp cooked bacon or turkey bacon, crumbled

Directions:

1. Combine chutney, honey, vinegar, mustard, salt, Worcestershire sauce,
   and oil in a blender and blend until mango chutney is chopped up.

2. Wash and spin-dry spinach.

3. Warm dressing in a saucepan over low heat.

4. Unless you have a very large salad bowl, divide spinach among
   two bowls to toss (or repeat a second time).

5. Coat spinach with some warm dressing and toss with part of the crumbled bacon (reserving half of it for garnish).

6. Serve salad on plates topped with remaining crumbled bacon.

NOTE: For a timesaving tip, add chutney to your child's favorite bottled French dressing.

CRUISE SHIP CAKE

This elegant cruise ship is easy to construct from a cake mix, canned frosting, candies, and snack cakes.

Ingredients:
1 package chocolate cake mix (or flavor of choice) prepared as directed
2 cans chocolate fudge frosting
1 can vanilla frosting
2 chocolate-glazed snack cake rolls
Lifesaver candies (original white mint flavor)
chocolate chips
4 one-half oz. tubes of red decorator's icing with round writing tip

Directions:

1. Preheat oven to 350°F (180°C).

2. Line a 9 x 13-inch cake pan with baking parchment and bake mix according to package directions for the pan size. Cool cake completely. Invert from pan and peel parchment paper from the bottom.

3. Cover a 12 x 20-inch sheet of cardboard with aluminum foil.

4. Cut cake as shown in diagram (Fig. 1).

5. Arrange pieces as shown in diagram (Fig. 2).

6. Grade down edges of ship at each end with a sharp knife (the bow and stern).

7. Cover the hull of the boat with a smooth layer of chocolate frosting.

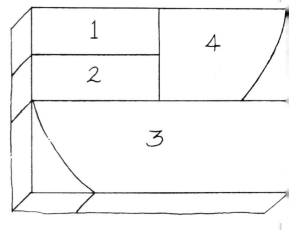

Fig. 1

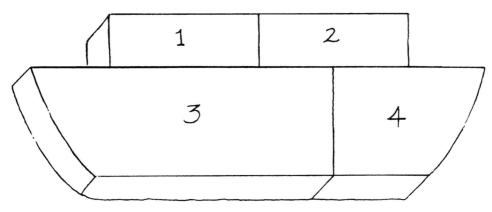

Fig. 2

8. Cover the deck and the topside of the ship with vanilla frosting.

9. Cut one snack cake in half and use the other whole. These will be steam stacks.

10. Arrange the whole one in front with the two halves (cut side against cake) behind them.

11. Use Lifesavers for portholes along the hull and chocolate chips for rows of windows topside.

12. Pipe red bands on the steam stacks with decorator's icing (*Fig. 3*). For the finishing touch, pipe S.S. (your daughter's name) on the side of the ship.

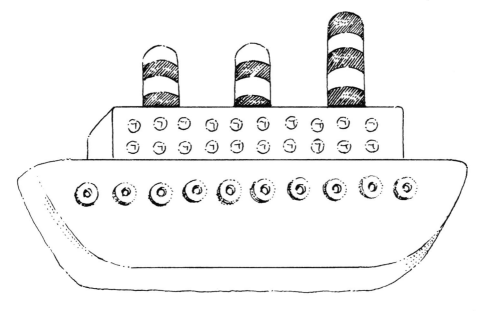

Fig. 3

ICE CREAM LIFE PRESERVERS

Ring molds hold about $4^1/_2$ cups liquid by volume. However, store-bought ice cream tends to be full of air. This recipe calls for buying a gallon, so that you'll have plenty of ice cream to pack down into the molds.

Ingredients:
unflavored nonstick cooking spray
1 gallon vanilla ice cream or frozen yogurt
2 three-quarter oz. tubes of blue decorator's gel

Directions:

1. Spray two $4^1/_2$-cup ring molds with nonstick cooking spray. (If you have only one mold, repeat the process.)

2. Pack ice cream into mold so that there will be no gaps, especially on the surface once the pans are inverted.

3. Freeze at least 8 hours.

4. Fill a baking pan with hot water.

5. Working quickly, dip molds in hot water and run a thin metal spatula around the edges if necessary.

6. Invert onto large, chilled plates and return to freezer for about an hour.

7. Use decorator's gel to write S.S. (your daughter's name) on each life preserver. Return to freezer for a least another hour before serving.

MOCK CHAMPAGNE IN ICE BUCKETS

Serve glass bottles of flavored sparkling water from a wine cooler or bucket filled with ice. For an authentic touch, replace the caps with corks and neatly fold napkins around the bottle necks the way champagne is presented in a fine restaurant. Pour into plastic champagne glasses and let the girls toast to a "Bon Voyage."

CRUISELINE CONTINENTAL BREAKFAST

In keeping with the life preserver theme, donuts are a natural choice for breakfast. Powdered sugar-covered donuts look the most like white life preservers. However, you can provide an assortment of donuts that includes glazed and chocolate-iced donuts. Your daughter can use a tube of decorator's icing to write S.S. (her name) across each donut . . . or let guests decorate their own donuts with their own names. Serve a selection of juices and milk to round out the morning meal.

MEDIEVAL PARTY

BOYS AND GIRLS AGES 8 TO 10

From King Arthur and Camelot to Druids and dragons, medieval parties set the stage for a fantasy-filled event. The party theme lends itself to both genders because it's just as appealing to young knights as it is to fairy-tale princesses.

Party Elements

Invitation: Shield of Chivalry

Decorations: Dragon signs, dragon footprints, shields, swords, flags, tapestries

Party Gear: Coronets and Barbettes

Instant Involvement: Fanfare

Games/Activities: In Search of the Golden Grail, Dragon Egg Hunt

Goody Bags: Dragon Bags

Invitation: Shield of Chivalry

A knight's shield was his most prized possession, as well as his means of protection. Even the stylized motifs served a practical purpose. Underneath all of that armor, it was pretty hard to tell one knight from the next.

MENU

ROAST LEGS
OF BEASTS

SWORDS IN STONES

GREEN DRAGON CAKE

ICE CREAM CASTLE

ELIXIR OF LIFE

The crests emblazoned across the front were often the only identifying symbols they had. Lions and leopards, crosses, crowns, and castles are some of the characters that frequently show up on shields. In a way, a knight's shield can be likened to a snowflake—no two are exactly alike. So why not personalize each invitation with a uniquely different design? You can assign a different shield to each knight (or lady) invited to your castle. Your child will love getting involved in this simple yet creative project.

Materials:
6 9 x 12-inch sheets of assorted colored construction paper
crayons
scissors, ruler, pencil
black felt-tip writing marker
12 envelopes large enough to fit $4^1/2$ x 6-inch cards
Makes 12 shields

Directions:
Each sheet of paper will make 2 cards. Use ruler and scissors to split each paper into two $4^1/2$ x 12-inch sheets. Fold each sheet in half and crease at the top (*Fig. 1*). Mark and trim the open ends of each card, together, forming the tapered point of a shield (*Fig. 2*).

Fig. 1

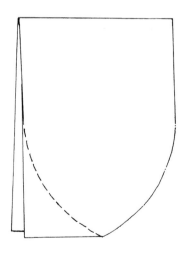

Fig. 2

On the inside of each shield, write the following message with the felt-tip marker (or use your computer or a photocopier to print out the invitation and cut to fit inside shields):

**COME TO THE CASTLE
NOBLE KNIGHTS AND LADIES FAIR**
for
FEASTING AND FESTIVITIES
at
THE GREAT ROUND TABLE
(address, time, date, and year given in the 500s A.D.)
RSVP (your phone number)

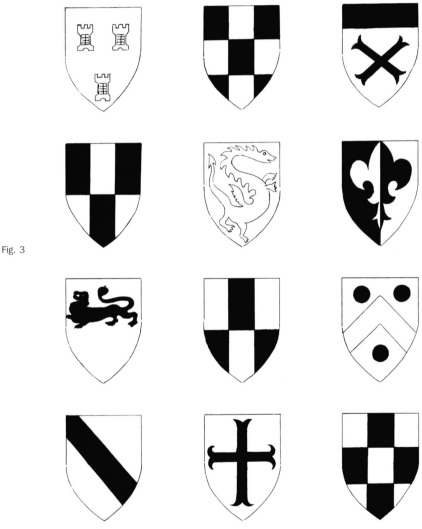

Fig. 3

Decorate shields as desired, using some of the examples (*Fig. 3*).
If desired, draw dragon tracks all over the envelopes, using green
crayons or markers.

Decorations

As the guests approach the party, you can put up some inviting signs like: BOTELER CASTLE AHEAD (obviously, you'd want to use your last name), DRAGON CROSSING, or BEWARE OF DRAGON. Use sidewalk chalk or washable tempera paint on your drive to make a path of dragon tracks to your door. Once inside, you can decorate the Great Hall of the castle with shields on the wall. It would be interesting to have shields represent-

ing those that you sent to the guests. After all, shield designs varied greatly and were very personalized. Make a collection of life-size cardboard shields and paint with some of the designs suggested in the invitation. Use felt sold by the roll and fabric paint to make long, bannerlike flags that can be hung from the ceiling. Paper cut from rolls can also work for this purpose. Another idea would be to hang a "tapestry" on the wall. Draw a medieval scene on a roll of brown paper and fill in with crayon, using a crosshatch effect. In fact, coloring the tapestry is something the kids can even do for an activity.

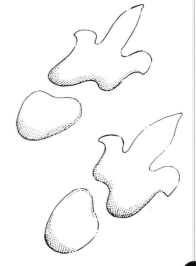

In keeping with King Arthur, you can always rent a tabletop extender from a party supply for a large "Round Table." Of course, Arthur's court was unique. Your castle could opt for the traditional, long banquet table. Decorate the table with toy dragons and action-figure dolls dressed in aluminum foil armor (your kids will have fun with that). The shield motif can be carried through with paper place markers and even drawn on paper plates with nontoxic crayons.

Party Gear: Coronets and Barbettes

A coronet is a crownlike cap worn by nobles below the rank of sovereign. When they were not in armor, lords and knights wore this less elaborate version of the king's headgear. Any jewels or precious stones were usually modest in comparison to the royal crown. Ladies of the medieval court wore barbettes. These tall, pointed hats resembled upside-down ice cream cones trimmed with ermine, jewels, and a sheer silk veil.

Coronet Materials:

1 20 x 30-inch poster board (any color)
gold or silver foil or foil wrapping paper
4 20 x 30-inch sheets red, royal blue, or purple crepe paper
large red, green, and blue sequins (for rubies, emeralds, and
    sapphires)
scissors, stapler, glue
Makes 12

Directions:

1. Cut poster board into
   12 1⁵/₈ x 30-inch strips.

2. Cover strips with foil or foil
   paper, securing in place with
   staples or glue.

3. Use your child's head as a model
   to adjust bands for proper fit.
   Staple bands into rings, overlapping ends.

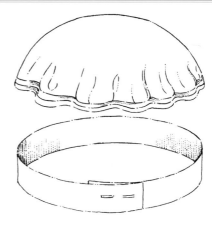

Fig. 1

4. Cut each sheet of crepe paper
   into 3 12-inch circles.

5. Tuck edges of circles around
   inside of bands and staple into
   place (*Fig. 1*). Decorate around
   bands by gluing on sequin jewels (*Fig. 2*).

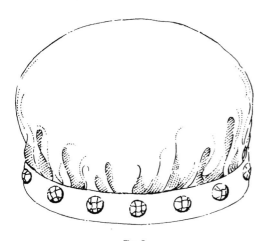

Fig. 2

Barbette Materials:

6 20 x 30-inch sheets of poster
  board (any color)
12 yds. netting or gauze
first-aid cotton on a roll, or fur cloth
large red, green, and blue sequins (for rubies, emeralds, and sapphires)
stapler, scissors, tape, glue
elastic bands
Makes 12

Directions:

1. Cut each sheet of poster board
   into a 20-inch circle.

2. Cut circles into semicircles.

3. Shape each semicircle into a
   cone and staple in place along
   the seam (*Fig. 3*).

Fig. 3

4. Cut off about $1/4$ inch from the tip of the hat to make a tiny hole.

5. Cut netting into 1-yd. pieces.

6. Gather a piece of netting at one end and pull through hole in each hat. Pull an inch of the netting through the hole and secure with tape on the inside.

7. Trim barbettes around the base by gluing on strips of "ermine" (cotton or fur cloth) and glue ruby, emerald, and sapphire sequins onto the fur trim (*Fig. 4*).

Fig. 4

8. Staple elastic hat bands at each side. (At times it can be awkward to walk around as a "cone head," so you might want to attach an elastic chin strap to secure hats in place.)

Instant Involvement: Fanfare

Anyone who's ever watched a medieval movie knows that those of noble rank are announced by resounding horns. For your party, a fanfare welcome will give each guest a special feeling of importance. It also helps to bridge that awkward stretch of time between the first and last arrival. Each child's grand entrance is greeted with royal regalia and the tantara of trumpets. As more children arrive, the larger and more impressive the ceremony becomes. Of course, at least two children must be present for the ceremony to begin. There should be one "harbinger" and several "heralders" (the more the merrier—as guests arrive, they get a horn and join the line). The ceremony commences when the first guest comes through the door. The harbinger reads the name of incoming guests from a large scroll, using a booming voice. The last name becomes the place of origin, for example: "Announcing Sir Thomas of Doughty or Lady Elizabeth of Warren." The heralders bring their horns to their mouth and either mock a "Toot Doodle Doo" with their voice or . . . you can get toy horns with kazoo-like mouthpieces. (Sound-effects tapes are also available; check with your public library.) The pageant continues until every child is present and accounted for. By the time the last guest arrives, the ceremony will have grown to pompous proportions. Since the early arrivals may feel somewhat cheated out of being fashionably late and getting all the glory and attention, have them enter all over again.

HERALDING HORNS

These can easily be fashioned out of cardboard tubes from leftover wrapping paper or long rolls of aluminum foil. You'll also need funnel-shaped plastic cups (like the kind that you snap into coffee mug holders), gold or silver foil, and crepe paper streamers (red, royal blue, or purple). Tape a cup to one end of each tube and mold foil tightly around the tube and cup. Heralding horns usually  had some kind of flag or streamers hanging from them. Just staple a long strip of crepe paper streamer around the base of the bell, cutting a V-shaped notch at the end of the streamer.

 # Games/Activities

IN SEARCH OF THE GOLDEN GRAIL

The quest for the Holy Grail was the underlying theme throughout the legend of King Arthur. It was a mission for only the noblest of knights—all others would fail. At the Round Table there was a special seat waiting for the finder of the Grail. It was called the Siege Perilous. For this game, you can make your own Golden

Grail using a little bit of Druid "alchemy" (turning base metals into gold). Instead of incantations, try gilding a metal or plastic goblet with gold paint, or wrapping it with gold foil. The Holy Grail was supposedly so radiant that it was covered with a cloth of white "samite" (silk) to shield the eyes of mere mortals. For this reason, you should drape a white handkerchief over the goblet. Now the Grail must be hidden in some brilliant place, either indoors or outside, weather permitting.

Arthurian lore presents many of life's problems in puzzling riddles; so does this game. You'll need to write up as many clues as you have players. They should be obscure. Examples: "The sun always shines brightest in the shade" would indicate that the Grail was hidden underneath a lamp. "Where the sea stands above the land" means that the Grail is in a birdbath. "In the belly of a water serpent" suggests that the Grail is in the coil of the garden hose. After all of the clues have been written on strips of paper, wad them up and put them in a "magic" box or bowl. Each knight (and lady) draws a clue and tries to solve the riddle. Only one clue is correct, so in theory, it will lead one knight to the Grail and the rest of the knights will be led on a wild-goose chase. However, clues can be misinterpreted, and there's always a chance that a knight in possession of the wrong clue might stumble across the Grail. It really doesn't matter. As legend goes, "destiny" determines who will take his rightful place in the Round Table's Siege Perilous.

DRAGON EGG HUNT

This medieval version of a classic egg hunt is a bounty hunt for dragon eggs as opposed to bunny eggs. Dye about 4 dozen hard-cooked eggs a pale green. (Make a solution of 2 cups boiling water, 2 tsp. white vinegar, and green food coloring.) Use a dark green marker to draw veins on the eggs. Hide eggs around the yard, in the house, or both. The game begins when a herald reads the king's proclamation from a scroll: "Hear ye, Hear ye . . . our kingdom is overrun with dragons, terrorizing the villagers and burning down cottages. Your Royal Highness has summoned you here today to gather all of the dragon eggs in the land and save us from another generation of destruction." Turn the kids loose with baskets or bags to collect as many eggs as they can. When all the eggs have been hunted down, they can be turned in for rewards. In general, each egg is worth a piece of gold and a precious gem (a chocolate coin and a giant gumdrop or jelly candy). The knight or lady who rids the kingdom of the most dragon eggs could qualify for a special prize . . . perhaps a toy dragon.

PHOTO OPS

After the knights and ladies have received their royal hats, have them make another "grand entrance" with fanfare as you snap pictures.

Goody Bags: Dragon Bags

Decorate shopping totes with "dragon tracks" or footprints. Fill bags with toy costume jewels or pendants (amulets), plastic or beanbag dragon toys, medieval comic or coloring books, and chocolate "dragon eggs." (Any candy eggs will do—also look for dinosaur candies that can pass for dragons.)

 # Recipes

ROAST LEGS OF BEASTS

Medieval feasts conjure up images of knights eating greasy hunks of meat with their hands and using their loyal dogs as napkins. To most kids, turkey legs look like they came from an enormous beast. In fact, don't be surprised if they can't finish them. You can always substitute chicken drumsticks, with thighs attached.

Ingredients:

12 turkey drumsticks
3 Tbs. unsalted butter, melted
3 Tbs. olive oil
2 Tbs. Worcestershire sauce
$1/4$ cup lemon juice
1 tsp. poultry seasoning
1 clove garlic, crushed
Makes 12 servings

Directions:

1. Preheat oven to 350°F (180°C). Lightly oil 2 9 x 13-inch baking pans or spray with nonstick spray (or use a very large roasting pan that can accommodate all of the drumsticks without crowding them).

2. Arrange drumsticks in the pan(s).

3. Combine butter, olive oil, Worcestershire sauce, lemon juice, poultry seasoning, and crushed garlic and brush over drumsticks.

4. Roast for 1 to $1^{1}/4$ hours, until skin is crisp and golden and juices run clear when pierced with a fork.

SWORDS IN STONES

As Arthurian legend goes, "Whoso shall pull the sword out of the stone is King of England by right." This prophecy was made by Merlin and fulfilled by young Arthur. Now, all the knights at your party can try their hand at this noble feat while they eat.

Ingredients:

12 baking potatoes
12 plastic knives
lightweight aluminum foil
WHIPPED CHIVE BUTTER (recipe follows)
Makes 12 servings

Directions:

1. Preheat oven to 375°F (190°C).

2. Scrub potatoes and place directly on oven rack. Bake 1 hour.

3. Meanwhile, make each sword as follows: Tear off 12 4 x 12-inch strips of aluminum foil.

4. Place a plastic knife lengthwise along the edge of each foil strip.

5. Roll up foil tightly around knife. Pinch foil to conform to the contour of the knife and flatten excess foil at the top.

6. Fold foil end over to form a handle for the sword, tucking the end around the knife.

7. Insert each sword into a hot baked potato. Serve with whipped chive butter.

WHIPPED CHIVE BUTTER

Ingredients:

1 cup unsalted butter or margarine, softened
$1/2$ cup sour cream
2 Tbs. snipped fresh chives

Directions:

1. Whip butter with an electric mixer until light and fluffy.

2. Beat in sour cream and chives. Serve in crocks or ramekins at the table.

GREEN DRAGON CAKE

Every dragon slayer knows that green dragons were the most common of the fire-breathing species, highly prized as a royal delicacy. In keeping with the green theme, this is a zucchini cake with tinted cream cheese frosting (similar to a carrot cake). You can also use any flavor of cake mix and canned frosting, tinted green.

Ingredients:

2 cups grated zucchini
$1/3$ cup boiling water
1 cup all-purpose flour
$1^1/4$ cups sugar
$1/2$ cup vegetable oil
$1^1/4$ tsp. baking soda
$1/2$ tsp. salt
1 tsp. cinnamon
1 tsp. ground cloves
1 tsp. nutmeg
1 tsp. vanilla extract
3 eggs
1 cup chopped walnuts
GREEN CREAM CHEESE FROSTING (recipe follows)
3 $3^1/2$-oz. trapezoid-shaped Swiss chocolate bars (Toblerone)
small black gumdrop
red licorice twist
pastry bag fitted with coupling nozzle and #10 round writing tip
Makes 12 generous servings

Come to the Castle
Ye Noble Knights
&
Ladies Faire
For
Feasting & Festivities
at
Ye Great Round Table

Ye Olde Pizza Parlor
Seventh Ave.
Camelot
Saturday, June 19th
In the year of 542 AD
At the hour when
the raven caws seven

RSVP
917 555 1212

Ice Cream Castle
(recipe pages 175–177)

Demonic Cat Cake
(recipe pages 192–194)

Directions:

1. Preheat oven to 350°F (180°C). Line 2 9-inch round cake pans with baking parchment.

2. Put zucchini in a mixing bowl and cover with boiling water. Let stand 5 minutes. Drain off water.

3. Add flour, sugar, oil, baking soda, salt, cinnamon, cloves, nutmeg, vanilla, and eggs.

4. Beat at medium speed for 3 minutes, scraping bowl occasionally.

5. Stir in walnuts.

6. Pour batter into prepared pans and bake 35 to 40 minutes, or until a toothpick inserted in center comes out clean.

7. Cool cakes completely. Turn cakes out of pans and peel away parchment.

8. Cover an 18 x 36-inch sheet of cardboard with foil.

9. Cut cake as in diagram (*Fig. 1*) and arrange on board as shown (*Fig. 2*).

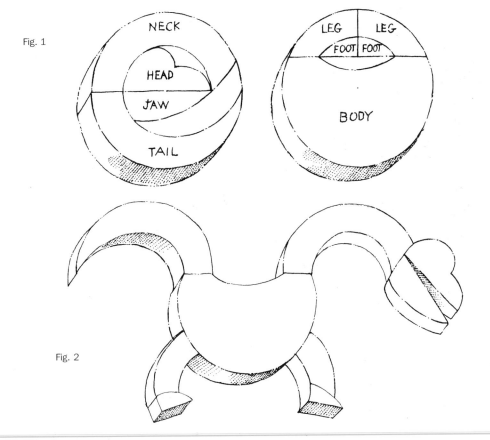

Fig. 1

Fig. 2

10. Frost cake with a smooth, even layer of frosting.

11. Fill pastry bag with remaining frosting. Pipe scales on body of dragon, beginning at the neck and working toward the tail.

12. Separate chocolate bars into triangular segments, using a sharp knife.

13. Insert chocolate segments to resemble scales running down the neck, back, and tail.

14. Use gumdrop for an eye. Split licorice twist at one end and insert uncut end into the mouth of the dragon (*Fig. 3*).

Fig. 3

GREEN CREAM CHEESE FROSTING

Ingredients:

1 cup unsalted butter or margarine, softened
4 oz. cream cheese, softened
8 cups powdered sugar
5 to 6 Tbs. lime or lemon juice
green paste or gel food coloring

Directions:

1. Beat butter and cream cheese together until light and fluffy.

2. Beat in powdered sugar and enough lime juice to make frosting a smooth and spreadable consistency.

3. Add a little bit of food coloring at a time, blending completely until you reach your desired shade of green.

ICE CREAM CASTLE

Ahh, ice cream castles—the stuff that dreams are made of! In keeping with this fantasy, it should be created out of your child's favorite flavor: from a realistic stone-colored mocha chip to a fairy-tale pink peppermint or pale green pistachio. The important thing is to select a brand of ice cream that comes packed in rectangular cartons and to keep it frozen very hard before assembling.

Ingredients:
2 half-gallon rectangular cartons of ice cream
  ($6^3/4$ x $4^3/4$ x $3^1/2$ inches)
1 pint of the same flavor of ice cream, for towers
1 three and one-half oz. chocolate bar with 6 scored segments
milk chocolate kisses and additional assorted candies
2 chocolate-flavored ice cream cones
Makes 12 servings

Directions:

1. Cover a 12 x 14-inch board with aluminum foil. Have chocolate bars at room temperature.

2. Using a very sharp, thin-bladed knife (it's helpful to heat it), cut each chocolate bar into one piece of 3 connected segments (for doors) and 3 individual segments (for windows).

3. Have ice cream frozen very hard. It may be necessary to return the castle to the freezer while you're working on it. Unwrap ice cream so that you have 2 solid blocks. Center one block on the foil so that it stands $4^3/4$ inches high. Slice the second block into 2 $6^3/8$ x $2^3/8$ x $4^3/4$-inch blocks.

4. Stand blocks on end, one on each side of the main ice cream block, for towers. If necessary, use toothpicks to secure blocks in place (*Fig. 1*).

5. Place a chocolate bar door in the center (front and back) of the castle. Put 3 windows across each side (front and back) of the castle. Line up chocolate kisses for battlements between towers.

6. Put a large scoop of ice cream on top of each tower, top with an inverted ice cream cone, and decorate with assorted candies (*Fig. 2*). Return to freezer until serving time.

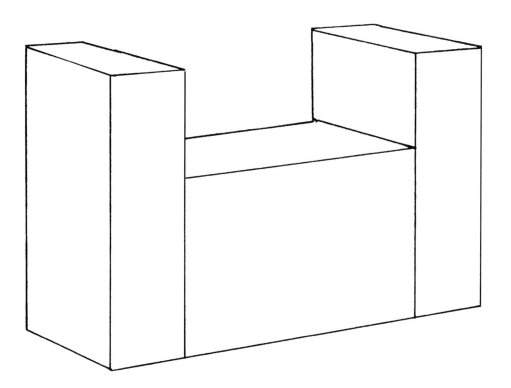

Fig. 1

Fig. 2

ELIXIR OF LIFE

The Druids believed there was a magical potion that could guarantee eternal youth and everlasting life. Its actual existence was as much of a quest as Arthur's search for the Holy Grail. Supposedly Merlin had sipped from this immortal brew, which was why he'd been around a long, long time. It's fun to imagine that you have bottles of the legendary liquid at your party. Serve grape juice in a large carafe and hang a sign around the neck that says "ELIXIR OF LIFE." Pour into goblets or mugs.

HOBGOBLIN GALA

ALL AGES—WITH ADJUSTMENTS FOR GAMES

Halloween actually began as an ancient Druid autumn festival called Samhain (pronounced *SAH win*), meaning summer's end. This Druid feast on fall harvest bounty is linked to the New World use of golden leaves, cornstalks, and pumpkins as decorations (the Druids used wheat stalks instead of corn and made jack o'lanterns out of turnips). Samhain night, the *hallowed eve* was the night before All Saints' Day. This was the night to lock the windows and bolt the door of your thatched cottage because all the *hobgoblins* from the spirit world were on the loose. (These ghosts, witches, fairies, and ugly little elves have been banging on front doors for centuries!)

Now Halloween is the season to don scary masks and run around the neighborhood on a candy raid. No wonder Halloween has become a favorite holiday even for us grown-up kids. It's a magical night when fantasy rules and we all become hobgoblins. Of course, some things have changed over the years. In many places, casual canvassing for candy has been replaced by supervised Halloween parties. This comes as no surprise to me. Back in the '60s, my parents began hosting annual Halloween parties. They were so much fun that as soon as we swept up the last kernel

MENU

PUMPKIN PIZZAS

HOBGOBLERS

DEMONIC CAT CAKE

ICE CREAM ARACHNIDS

GHOULISH GREEN
APPLE CIDER

of candy corn, we were already planning the menu and games for the following year. This family ritual became as big a tradition as our Thanksgiving turkey dinner. Those parties left a legacy of memories that I will always cherish.

 # Party Elements

Invitation: Pumpkin Popcorn Ball

Decorations: Hobgoblin greeting signs, ghost tree, sidewalk luminaries, "Enter Sanctum," ghouloons, jack o'lantern balloons and plates, leaf-lined floor

Party Gear: Spider Head Hats

Instant Involvement: Masquerade Magic

Games/Activities: Ghost Busting with Jumping Jack o'Lanterns, Pumpkin Piñata Punching, Tales from the Crypt

Goody Bags: Stuffed Pumpkins

 # Invitation: Pumpkin Popcorn Ball

In keeping with the trick-or-treat tradition, I find that an edible invitation is a big hit for Halloween parties. Since most of the guests are either neighbors or school friends, a "special delivery" by hand is usually not a problem. If a few have to be mailed, they're lightweight and fit nicely into a small box with some extra popcorn for packing peanuts.

Materials:
12 PUMPKIN POPCORN BALLS (recipe follows), or
   use store-bought orange popcorn balls and insert
   cinnamon sticks for stems
4 sheets of 9 x 12-inch orange construction paper
ruler, scissors, black felt-tip calligraphy pen, hole punch
black curling ribbon
12 12-inch squares orange or clear cellophane
Makes 12 invitations

Directions:

1. Cut each sheet of construction paper into 3 4 x 9-inch pieces. You will have 12 strips of paper.

2. Use pen to write the following invitation in a long column down each strip:

**Announcing a Hobgoblin Gala
in Celebration of Samhain Night**
at (your address)
on (date) at (time)
"Come as You Aren't!"
RSVP (your phone number)
(have your child sign his or her name)

(Note: many Halloween parties are not actually held on Halloween)

3. Fold each paper up accordion style, creasing at 1-inch intervals (*Fig. 1*).

4. Punch a hole in the corner (*Fig. 2*).

5. For each pumpkin: Wrap a sheet of cellophane around popcorn ball. Secure in place by tying a 12-inch length of curling ribbon in a knot around the cinnamon stick stem.

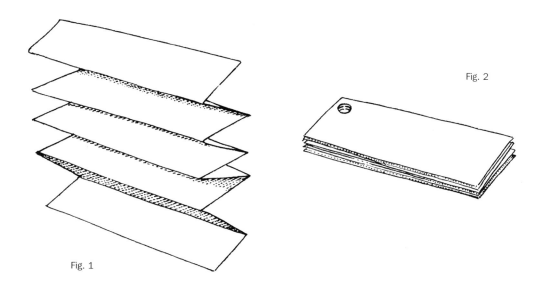

Fig. 2

Fig. 1

6. Thread ribbon through hole in invitation and tie again. Curl ends of ribbon with scissors (*Fig. 3*).

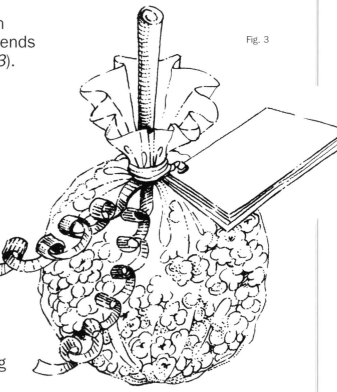

Fig. 3

PUMPKIN POPCORN BALLS

Ingredients:
9 cups popped popcorn
$1/2$ cup sugar
$1/2$ cup light corn syrup
$1/2$ cup water
1 tsp. white vinegar
$1/2$ tsp. salt
2 tsp. grated orange peel
$3/4$ cup butter or margarine,
  softened
1 tsp. vanilla extract
$1/2$ tsp. orange extract
orange paste or gel food coloring
12 whole cinnamon sticks
Makes 12

Directions:

1. Place popcorn in a very large bowl. Combine sugar, corn syrup, water, vinegar, salt, and orange peel in a 2-quart saucepan with a candy thermometer hooked onto the side.

2. Heat to boiling over medium heat, stirring constantly, until mixture reaches 260°F (127°C) or until a drop of the mixture poured into ice water forms a hard ball.

3. Remove from heat and stir in butter, vanilla, and orange extract.

4. Stir enough food coloring into syrup to make it bright orange (color will fade somewhat when syrup is added to white popcorn).

5. Pour syrup over popcorn in a thin stream and gently stir with a buttered wooden spoon.

6. When cool enough to touch but still warm, shape popcorn mixture into 4-inch balls. (Use buttered hands to make the job easier.)

7. Push a cinnamon stick into each ball for pumpkin stem. Place on buttered foil to cool. You may refrigerate the popcorn balls for about 20 minutes to speed hardening.

Decorations

Fig. 1

I love the use of roadside and yard signs for theme parties. I think they're a must-have decoration for Halloween. The first sign leading up to the house can be a bedsheet ghost formed over a cross of signposts (stuff the head a little) and tied with cord; draw a face with a laundry marker. Use an old, weathered-looking board to make a "HOBGOBLIN HOUSE AHEAD" sign

Fig. 2

and nail it to the cross post (*Fig. 1*). The next sign could be "BLACK CAT XING" (*Fig. 2*). After all, nobody wants a black cat crossing their path. The final sign should go at the end of the driveway: a skull and crossbones with a "DEAD END" sign, again made from weathered wood (*Fig. 3*).

Where I live in Connecticut, "ghost trees" on Halloween have become as classic as candles in the windows at Christmastime. On every street, you see house after house with those grade-school handkerchief-style ghosts hanging from a front tree. At night, they're enhanced with strings of twinkling white lights. I also like to paint pumpkin faces on orange plastic plates with glow-in-the-dark yellow paint. Hang plates from the tree, using brown cord to look like stems (*Fig. 4*)

Fig. 3

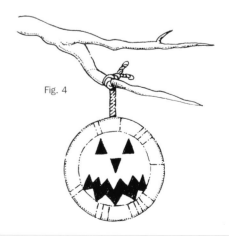

Fig. 4

Line the sidewalk or driveway with luminaries to greet guests; use hollowed-out gourds or mini-pumpkins and put votive candles inside. You could even do it "Druid style" and carve out turnips! Make spiders with wads of tissue paper and pipe-cleaner legs. Cover the door with store-bought spider webbing and stick spiders all over the door. Put a weathered sign on the door that says: "ENTER SANCTUM."

Once inside, I like to bring the outdoors in. Cover the floor of the party room with black plastic paint dropcloths. Rake up those autumn leaves into lawn bags and dump them in the party room, spreading them around on the floor. Decorate the walls with leafy branches and put bundles of cornstalks in the corners, adding pumpkins and gourds. Hang "ghouloons" from the ceiling: Drape white, gauzelike fabric over white balloons and gently draw faces with a marker. You can also use a marker to give orange balloons jack o'lantern faces (*Fig. 5*). Spread the party table with a black tablecloth, then cover with spider webbing. Decorate orange cups and plates with jack o'lantern faces. Fill a big black kettle or Dutch oven with candy corn and put it in the middle of the table. For place cards: Bake large tombstone cookies cut from gingerbread dough (or use ready-made sugar cookie dough). Decorate with frosting to identify each guest (*Fig. 6*). Be sure to have the Spider Head Hats waiting at the table.

Fig. 5

Fig. 6

Party Gear: Spider Head Hats

A Halloween party is one affair where costumes are a given. Even though most kids will have their own headgear of some kind, they'll still love these goofy-looking spider hats.

Materials:

2 pkgs. (40 20 x 30-inch sheets) black tissue paper
12 rubber bands
24 paper plates
24 three-quarter inch round white pressure-sensitive labels (for eyes)
2 rolls black crepe paper streamers
12 mask bands (or use black elastic cord from a fabric shop)
Black felt-tip marker, transparent tape, stapler

Directions:

1. For each spider hat, wad up a sheet of tissue into a tight ball.

2. Crisscross two sheets of tissue and place ball in the center (*Fig. 1*).

3. Gather tissue around ball and secure with rubber band to form a spider head (*Fig. 2*).

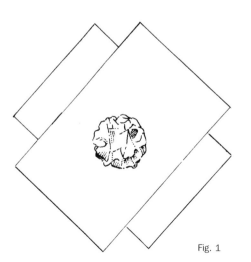

Fig. 1

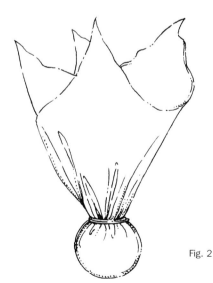

Fig. 2

4. Stack two paper plates together and place in front of you so that the bottoms of the plates are facing up. Center spider head in the middle of the top plate.

5. Turn paper under plate and staple around edges (*Fig. 3*).

6. Turn hat over and tape down loose paper with an X of tape.

7. Staple mask band or strips of elastic cord to opposite edges of plate for a neck strap.

8. Cut 4 strips of crepe paper streamers, each 2 yards in length.

9. Hold streamers together and tie around spider head to make 4 long legs that hang over each side.

10. Tie a knot at end of each leg.

11. Stick a pair of labels on head and add pupils with marker (*Fig. 4*).

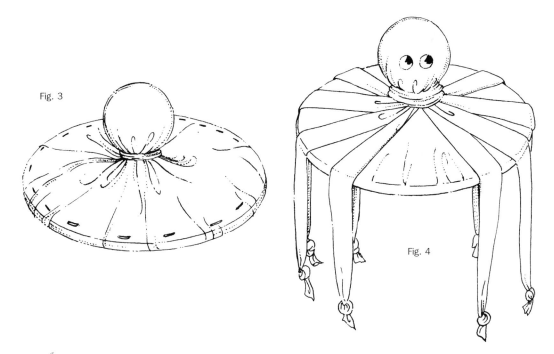

Fig. 3

Fig. 4

Instant Involvement: Masquerade Magic

As with party hats, many children will be coming to a Halloween party already wearing masks . . . but that doesn't keep them from wanting a second one. These fancy masquerade-type masks are reminiscent of those worn in the French court or at Mardi Gras in New Orleans. They're simply held up in front of the face whenever a guest wishes to obscure his or her identity from another guest (a least that's the historical intent). The real fun comes from making your own—glue-on sequins, glitter, and feathers make these a do-it-yourself fashion statement.

Materials:

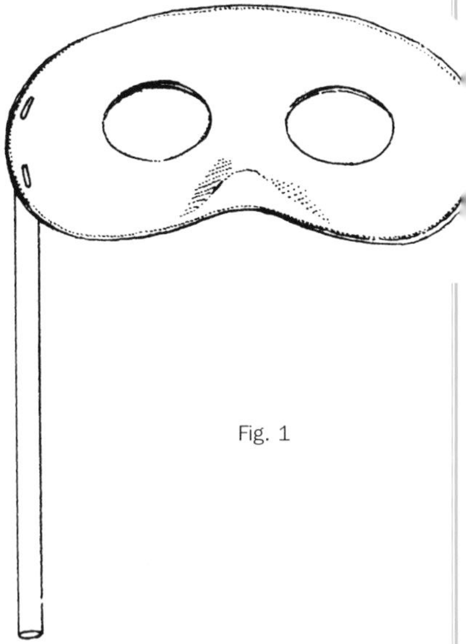

12 half masks on sticks (*Fig. 1*)
(*Note:* These are available at party supply
    stores. If you can't find any with sticks, you
    can staple them to sanded, painted pieces
    of dowel.)
craft glue (have several bottles so kids won't
    have to wait their turn)
assorted feathers (offer both colored and nat-
    ural)
sequins
glitter
Makes 12 masks

Fig. 1

Directions:

1. Have a craft table set up, ready and waiting for the guests as
    they arrive. Arrange feathers and sequins in bowls and dishes
    along with glitter shakers.

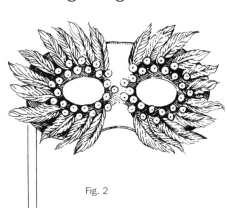

2. Give each child a mask and show
    him or her how to use the various
    media to create different effects
    (*Fig. 2*). Be sure to label masks
    while they dry during the party;
    "who made what" is always a
    very important issue.

Fig. 2

Games/Activities

GHOST BUSTING WITH JUMPING JACK O'LANTERNS

This is a fun, active game that works well against a garage door or a sturdy recreation room wall. First you'll need to make "balloon head" ghosts: Fill 2 or 3 dozen balloons with about 6 pieces of candy corn each. Inflate balloons so that they're tight enough to break from impact, but not so tight that they'll pop from handling. Drape a sheet of tissue over each balloon and tie around the "neck" with some black or orange ribbon. Add eyes and mouth with black marking pen (*Fig. 1*). Use

Fig. 1

markers to decorate two orange tennis balls to look like jack o'lanterns (*Fig. 2*). Tape or tack ghost balloons to a wall or garage

door. Have kids line up to take turns breaking the balloon ghosts. Each child gets two shots, so there should be at least two balloon ghosts per party guest (you may have to add some more as you go along). Players keep taking turns until all of the ghosts are "busted." (Kids really love watching the candy corn fly out of their heads!)

Fig. 2

PUMPKIN PIÑATA PUNCHING

I love piñatas as party games, except for one thing—if the first player breaks it, the game's over fast. Having multiple papier mâché piñatas can be either expensive to buy or time consuming to make. Fashioned from crepe paper, this simple version of a pumpkin piñata is practical enough that you can have several: For each piñata, fill a brown paper lunch bag with some Halloween candy and air-popped popcorn. Tape it shut and wrap several layers of wadded tissue paper around it. Place tissue ball in the center of a sheet of orange crepe paper and bring up sides of tissue, twisting at the top. Wrap twisted top with floral tape, making a loop that's bound back into the stem. Depending on the number of party guests, make 1 piñata for every 3 or 4 players. Tie a rope through the stem loop of the piñata and hang from a tree limb, beam, or hook on the ceiling. Move the piñata up and down while players take turns being blindfolded and swinging a broom at the bobbing pumpkin. Give each player 3 strikes before moving on to the next.

As soon as the piñata breaks, replace it with the next one. Keep going until everyone's had a fair chance to "punch a pumpkin."

TALES FROM THE CRYPT

For this game you'll need a big appliance box or a couple of large boxes that you can tape together to construct a crypt with a lid that flips open (it need not be claustrophobically small). Spray-paint it with one of the new faux-finish paints that look like granite or marble. On the side write "HERE LIES . . ." Make slips of paper with the names of famous deceased people (be sure they'd be familiar to the age group of the party guests). Put slips of paper in a dry vase holding some artificial flowers. Place the vase at the foot of the crypt and dim the lights. Kids sit in a circle around the crypt. The first player pulls a slip of paper from the vase and reads the name, keeping it to himself. The player gets inside the crypt, and the guessing game begins. Kids take turns, going around the circle, each asking a question that might offer a clue as to the person's identity. The player answers the questions from inside the box. Obviously, one rule is that a question cannot directly ask the identity of the deceased (for example: "Are you George Washington?"). The first player to guess the identity as a result of his or her question gets the next turn inside the box.

PHOTO OPS

Some "Kodak moments" include a close-up mug shot of each child as they make their entrance in costume or swinging a broom at a pumpkin piñata. Great group photos to take: Kids making and trying on their masquerade masks or "ghost busting" with jumping jack o'lanterns.

 # Goody Bags: Stuffed Pumpkins

Purchase orange gift sacks (lunch bag size) from a party shop. Fill with Halloween candies, lollipops dressed up like ghosts, Halloween theme erasers, mini-flashlights, chattering teeth. . . Twist tops of bags shut and wrap with floral tape to look like a pumpkin stem.

 # Recipes

PUMPKIN PIZZAS

These biscuit crust pizzas look like pumpkins with jack o'lantern faces. You can prebake the crusts ahead of time and do the final baking right before serving.

Ingredients:

2 16.3-oz. cans jumbo biscuits (8 to a can)
1 12-oz. bottle chili sauce
1 lb. (4 cups) grated cheddar cheese
pitted ripe olives
Makes 12 pizzas

Directions:

1. Preheat oven to 375°F (190°C). Open cans of biscuits and separate.

2. Use 12 biscuits for crusts and reserve 4 for making stems. Divide biscuits among 3 large baking sheets so that there are 4 well-spaced biscuits on each sheet.

3. Pat and flatten out the biscuits until they are stretched into 5 x 6-inch ovals (*Fig. 1*).

4. Rework ovals slightly so that they're pumpkin-shaped (*Fig. 2*).

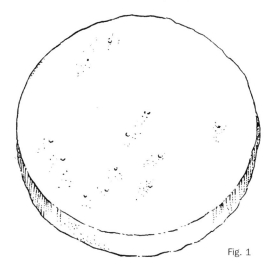

Fig. 1

Fig. 2

5. Cut each of the remaining biscuits into strips and shape into stems (*Fig. 3*).

6. Press stems into pumpkins and partially bake 6 minutes, or until dough is set but not browned. (You can prepare crusts a day or 2 in advance to this point and keep refrigerated.)

7. Spread each crust with about a tablespoon of chili sauce.

8. Cover each pizza with $1/3$ cup grated cheese (except for stem).

9. Split olives in half and cut into triangles (*Fig. 4*). Decorate pizzas to resemble jack o'lanterns.

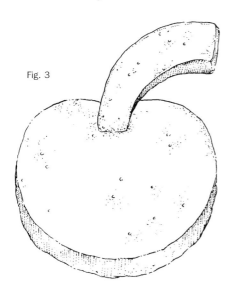

Fig. 3

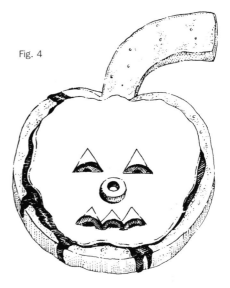

Fig. 4

10. Continue to bake at 375°F (190°C) about 6 to 10 minutes longer, or until cheese is melted and crust is golden. (*Note:* If stems get too brown, you can cover them with small pieces of foil while baking.) Serve immediately.

HOBGOBLERS

Put this platter of munchies on the party table to satisfy both big-time snackers and picky eaters—you know, the kids who never eat a meal that's placed in front of them.

Devil's Dip

Combine equal parts softened cream cheese and mild salsa. Serve in hollowed-out mini pumpkins.

Witches' Hats

Bugle-shaped corn snacks. (You can also use cheddar-flavored chips for an orange accent.)

Broomsticks

Pretzel rods.

Celery Sweepers

Cut several bunches of celery stalks into equal lengths. Cut a row of $1^1/2$-inch-long gashes, at the end of each stalk. Soak in ice water for several hours, or until ends fan out like brooms.

DEMONIC CAT CAKE

Throughout the ages, our feline friends have been either revered or feared. In ancient Egypt, they were worshipped in temples. The Druids believed that cats had once been human beings who were changed into that form for doing evil deeds. In Colonial times, cats were burned at the stake with witches. The settlers of Salem, Massachusetts, were suspicious of cats' eyes. After all, they glowed in the dark as if Satan were staring back at them. Kids will get a big kick out of this Halloween cat cake when you turn down the lights. Its fiery eyes make it seem positively possessed!

Ingredients:

EASY PUMPKIN CAKE (recipe follows) or use any chocolate cake recipe
    or mix
MIDNIGHT CHOCOLATE BUTTERCREAM FROSTING (recipe follows)
Slivered almonds
1 chocolate kiss
black licorice laces
2 lengthwise eggshell halves from a *small* egg
2 sugar cubes
pastry bag with coupling nozzle
Makes 12 generous servings

Directions:

1. Cover a 15 x 20-inch sheet of cardboard with foil.

2. Cut cake as shown in diagram (*Fig. 1*) and arrange on board (*Fig. 2*).

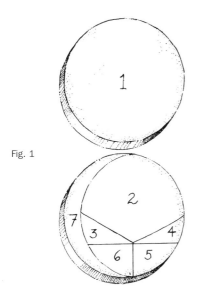

Fig. 1

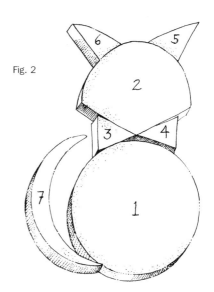

Fig. 2

3. Join all parts and frost top and sides of cake with chocolate butter-cream frosting.

4. Fill pastry bag fitted with a coupling nozzle with the remaining frosting (there's no need for a decorating tip). Pipe brow, cheeks, and paws as shown (*Fig. 3*).

5. Insert almond slivers for teeth and claws. Use chocolate kiss for nose and pieces of licorice lace for whiskers.

6. Set eggshells in place for eyes or use gumdrops for eyes (*Fig. 4*).

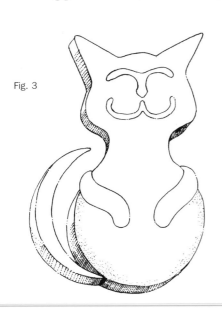

Fig. 3

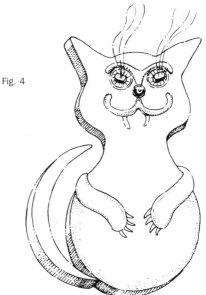

Fig. 4

7. Just before serving, put a sugar cube in each eggshell, saturate with lemon extract, and light with a match. Be sure to dim the lights and wait for the OOOHs and AAAHs!

EASY PUMPKIN CAKE

Ingredients:

1 box yellow cake mix
1 16-oz. can solid-pack pumpkin
2 tsp. baking soda
$1^1/_2$ tsp. cinnamon
$1^1/_2$ tsp. pumpkin pie spice
2 eggs
$1/_3$ cup water
Makes 2 9-inch layers

Directions:

1. Preheat oven to 350°F (180°C). Line 2 9-inch round cake pans with baking parchment.

2. Combine cake mix, pumpkin, baking soda, cinnamon, pumpkin pie spice, eggs, and water in a large mixing bowl.

3. Beat at low speed for 30 seconds. Scrape down bowl, then beat at medium speed for 4 minutes.

4. Divide batter evenly between pans and bake 40 to 45 minutes.

5. Cool cakes completely. Invert pans and remove baking parchment from bottom of cakes.

MIDNIGHT CHOCOLATE BUTTERCREAM FROSTING

Ingredients:

6 cups powdered sugar
1 cup cocoa powder
1 cup unsalted butter or margarine, softened
1 tsp. vanilla
6 Tbs. water
Black paste or gel food coloring (optional)

Directions:

1. Combine powdered sugar, cocoa, butter, vanilla, and half of water in a large mixing bowl.

2. Blend ingredients at low speed.

3. Beat in enough of the remaining water to make frosting a smooth, creamy consistency.

4. Tint frosting slightly darker with a small amount of black food coloring.

ICE CREAM ARACHNIDS

These frozen spiders will send chills up anyone's spine. Their chocolate-coconut-covered bodies and long licorice legs make them look like tarantulas!

Ingredients:

1 14-oz. pkg. flaked coconut
3 Tbs. Dutch process cocoa powder
1 gallon chocolate ice cream
24 miniature chocolate chips (or raisins) for eyes
48 black licorice twists (for legs)
Large ice cream scoop (#20 food scoop)
Small ice cream scoop (#100 food scoop)
Makes 12 servings

Directions:

1. Combine coconut and cocoa powder in a large zip-lock bag. Shake until coconut is completely chocolate coated.

2. Cover a tray with foil. Make 12 large scoops and 12 small scoops of ice cream and place on tray. Put ice cream scoops back in the freezer for about 30 minutes so that ice cream will be easier to handle.

3. Remove tray from freezer. Place coconut in a pie plate. (You may want to use just half of it at a time so it doesn't mix with melting ice cream.)

4. Roll large scoops of ice cream in coconut and place on a tray lined with a clean sheet of foil.

5. Press small scoops of coconut against large scoops and use miniature chocolate chips or raisins for eyes (*Fig. 1*). Return to freezer until serving time.

6. Just before serving, cut licorice twists in half and place 4 halves on each side of the body, bending to resemble legs (*Fig. 2*).

NOTE: I prefer adding the licorice at the last minute because licorice tends to crack in the freezer.

Fig. 1

Fig. 2

GHOULISH GREEN APPLE CIDER

Kids love drinking this green-colored apple cider with squiggly gelatin floating around in it. You can use small Halloween cutters or simply cut it into squares. Be sure you buy pasteurized apple juice for this recipe. Fresh apple cider is too dark and cloudy to tint green.

Ingredients:

3 half-gallons apple juice
4 boxes white grape gelatin
green liquid or gel food coloring
Makes 12 generous servings

Directions:

1. Open bottles of apple juice and add a few drops of color to each. (Be sure all bottles are the same shade.) Chill.

2. Heat $2^1/2$ cups of the apple juice and dissolve gelatin in it. Pour into a 9 x 13-inch pan and chill until firm.

3. Cut gelatin into cubes or Halloween shapes and divide among cups. Pour apple juice over gelatin and serve.

INDEX

CONVERSION TABLES

SOLID MEASURES

For cooks measuring items by weight, here are approximate equivalents, in both Imperial and metric. So as to avoid awkward measurements, some conversions are not exact.

	U.S. CUSTOMARY	METRIC	IMPERIAL
Butter	1 cup	225 g	8 oz
	1/2 cup	115 g	4 oz
	1/4 cup	60 g	2 oz
	1 Tbsp	15 g	1/2 oz
Cheese (grated)	1 cup	115 g	4 oz
Fruit (chopped fresh)	1 cup	225 g	8 oz
Herbs (chopped fresh)	1/4 cup	7 g	1/4 oz
Meats/Chicken (chopped, cooked)	1 cup	175 g	6 oz
Mushrooms (chopped, fresh)	1 cup	70 g	2 1/2 oz
Nuts (chopped)	1 cup	115 g	4 oz
Raisins (and other dried chopped fruits)	1 cup	175 g	6 oz
Rice (uncooked)	1 cup	225 g	8 oz
(cooked)	3 cups	225 g	8 oz
Vegetables (chopped, raw)	1 cup	115 g	4 oz

LIQUID MEASURES

The Imperial pint is larger than the U.S. pint; therefore, note the following when measuring liquid ingredients.

U.S.	IMPERIAL
1 cup = 8 fluid ounces	1 cup = 10 fluid ounces
1/2 cup = 4 fluid ounces	1/2 cup = 5 fluid ounces
1 tablespoon = 3/4 fluid ounce	1 tablespoon = 1 fluid ounce

U.S. MEASURE	METRIC APPROXIMATE	IMPERIAL APPROXIMATE
1 quart (4 cups)	950 mL	1 1/2 pints + 4 Tbsp
1 pint (2 cups)	450 mL	3/4 pint
1 cup	236 mL	1/4 pint + 6 Tbsp
1 Tbsp	15 mL	1+ Tbsp
1 tsp	5 mL	1 tsp

DRY MEASUREMENTS

Outside the United States, the following items are measured by weight. Use the following table, but bear in mind that measurements will vary, depending on the variety of flour and moisture. Cup measurements are loosely packed; flour is measured directly from package (presifted).

	U.S. CUSTOMARY	METRIC	IMPERIAL
Flour (all-purpose)	1 cup	150 g	5 oz
Cornmeal	1 cup	175 g	6 oz
Sugar (granulated)	1 cup	190 g	$6^{1}/2$ oz
(confectioners)	1 cup	80 g	$2^{2}/3$ oz
(brown)	1 cup	160 g	$5^{1}/3$ oz

OVEN TEMPERATURES

Fahrenheit	225	300	350	400	450
Celsius	110	150	180	200	230
Gas Mark	$1/4$	2	4	6	8

EMERGENCY SUBSTITUTIONS

IF YOU DON'T HAVE	SUBSTITUTE
1 cup cake flour	1 cup minus 2 tablespoons all-purpose flour
1 tablespoon cornstarch (for thickening)	2 tablespoons all purpose flour
1 teaspoon baking powder	1/4 teaspoon baking soda plus 1/2 cup buttermilk or sour milk (to replace 1/2 cup of the liquid called for in the recipe)
1 package active dry yeast	1 cake compressed yeast
1 cup granulated sugar	1 cup packed brown sugar or 2 cups sifted powdered sugar
1 cup honey	1 1/4 cups granulated sugar plus 1/2 cup water
1 square (1 ounce) unsweetened chocolate	3 tablespoons unsweetened cocoa powder plus 1 tablespoon margarine or butter
1 cup buttermilk	1 tablespoon lemon juice or vinegar plus whole milk to make 1 cup. Let stand 5 minutes before using.
1 cup whole milk	1/2 cup evaporated milk plus 1/2 cup water or 1 cup reconstituted nonfat dry milk plus 1 1/2 teaspoons margarine or butter
1 cup half-and-half	1 cup minus 2 tablespoons whole milk plus 2 tablespoons margarine or butter
1 teaspoon finely grated lemon peel	1/2 teaspoon lemon extract